D1871164

MOTIVATION– THE ESSENCE OF LIVING

MOTIVATION–THE ESSENCE OF LIVING

Dr Viswanathan Gopalan

GenNext Publication

©Author

All rights reserved. No part of this work may be reproduced, stored, adapted, or transmitted in any form or by any means, electronic, mechanical, photocopying, micro-filming recording or otherwise, or translated in any language, without the prior written permission of the copyright owner and the publisher. The book is sold subject to the condition that it shall not, by way of trade or otherwise, be lent, resold, hired out, or otherwise circulated without the prior publisher's written consent in any form of binding or cover other than that in which it is published.

The views and opinions expressed in this book are author(s) own and the facts reported by them have been verified to the extent possible, and the publishers are not in any way liable for the same.

ISBN: 978-93-8022-253-0

Price: ₹ 190/-

Published by

Gennext Publishing House
23, Main Ansari Road, Daryaganj,
New Delhi-110002
Phone : 23282060, 23261060 Fax : (011) 23285914

Laser Typesetting: Lucky Graphic, Delhi
Printed at: Chowla Offset Printer, Delhi

Cataloging in Publication Data—DK
Courtesy: D.K. Agencies (P) Ltd. <docinfo@dkagencies.com>

Gopalan, Viswanathan, author.
Motivation - the essence of living / Dr Viswanathan Gopalan.
pages ; cm
Includes bibliographical references (pages).
ISBN 9789380222530

1. Motivation (Psychology) 2. Life. I. Title.

DDC 153.8 23

CONTENTS

Acknowledgements

I acknowledge and thank all my friends, students and colleagues in the Educational Institutions in Pune where I have taught over the last several years of my career, the fellow researchers whom I meet in conferences, who sincerely wished that I should publish the first book of my choice which I had been promising to write for many years and could make it happen now. Their constant reminders have been inspiring and definitely motivating to help me enter the world of book writing.

Special thanks and appreciation to my loved ones and family members including my dear wife Indira, daughter Sharmila, her husband Arjun and my son Vivek who constantly lent me support and their words of appreciation kept me inspired to finish my job well.

I wish to thank N Krishnaswamy, ex-IPS officer of excellence and eminence, Founder, Chairman, Mentor ,Vidya Vrikshah, the NGO in Chennai, serving the cause of helping and educating the Visually Challenged Children of India, who was kind enough to write the foreword for the book and suggest recommendations for its improvement.

It will not be appropriate if I do not acknowledge the initiative shown and the support given by B P Garg, Director, Gyan Books Pvt Ltd, New Delhi, in ensuring publication of this book by his company. I wish to thank all memebers of his team from production, publication and marketing who lent active support for the objective.

I wish to congratulate and thank all the readers who read, enjoy and stand to benefit from this book, in leading a more motivated and inspired life of purpose and vision.

I thank God for giving me this opportunity to serve Humanity by sharing the thoughts I had on this subject in which I have managed to acquire knowledge, with His Blessings and Grace.

Viswanathan Gopalan 04-09-2014

Pune, India

Foreword

Modern day living has become complicated. With all the advances of technology and comforts surrounding us in every walk of life, we still face challenges of coping and staying focussed and happy. Stress is an issue affecting not only the meek and the poor, but the wealthy, the powerful and the mighty. Everyone including leaders of nations, leaders of religions and leaders in the field of academia, wonder how peace and happiness can be brought about among people aspiring to enjoy them in their life time.

In this book, "Motivation–The Essence of Living", Dr Viswanathan Gopalan, firmly proposes that for facing these challenges of today, the key answer is Motivation. Through the uncertainties, the ups and downs which each one of us individually and collectively face, we need to look at the possibilities of how we can attain growth, prosperity, happiness and peace, staying motivated along the route.

Dr Viswanathan Gopalan has been an engineer, a corporate manager, a professor in management, a trainer, a research and he has also been associated with our Social Service Organisation. This book on motivation, written by him, can be read and appreciated by the academic and research communities, organisations in the public and private domain, and NGOs serving the people in all fields. What he has to say is interesting, enabling and inspiring.

I am sure the reader of this book will benefit immensely in terms of knowledge and value while he enjoys reading this book.

N. Krishnaswamy July 15, 2014
(Rtd.-IPS)
Founder- chairman Vidya Vrikshah

Introduction

'Live as if you were to die tomorrow. Learn as if you were to live forever.'

Mahatma Gandhi

'Try not to become a man of success but a man of value.'

Albert Einstein

Motivation–The Key to Living Life Well and Happy

The problem everyone faces in life today is unhappiness despite all the comforts and pleasures, modern day living has brought to us. We are confronted with stress, tension and resulting loss of will to live happily. Many are not aware of this. Even if they do, there is very little they think they can do about it. They go on struggling, trying to accumulate wealth and other possessions hoping it will bring joy and peace in their lives some day.

I want to share in this book with all of you, the secrets to living and leading a life of happiness, joy and peace regardless of the ups and downs of life, the hurdles, the challenges one needs to surmount. I have thought, I had searched, researched and have stumbled upon the truth. The truth according to me is 'Stay Motivated Always'.

Motivation is the key. It doesn't matter how many things you own, how much money you make, or how important people think you are. If you don't learn how to stay motivated to enjoy your life, no amount of wealth or absence of it in the name of sacrifice, will bring you the happiness, content and joy you are looking for.

Let me share with you a story to illustrate the point I am trying to convince you about.

The Story of a Tennis Player

Thomas Muster (Ref B. 8, B. 9), born in Austria in the year 1937, is one of the greatest clay court Tennis players the world has known in modern times. When he played his best game on clay at the age of 22, the barrel chested Austrian harnessed tremendous balance off both wings to wear down his rivals with heavy topspin shots. Thomas Muster ranks as one of the best clay court players of all time.

Tragedy struck the luminous, budding career of this young player in a strange and cruel manner. On 1st April 1989, in his fifth season as a professional player, Muster found himself in hospital, just two hours after he had come back from two sets down to beat World No. 13 Yannick Noah to reach the final of a tournament in Miami. His career had been on an upward trajectory till then. On that fateful day he became the victim of a Truck driven by a reckless driver. He was severely injured and had his cruciate and side ligaments in his left knee totally damaged and torn which left him a cripple unable to walk properly.

Muster flew back to Vienna for surgery, thinking he would make a quick recovery. Doctors weren't so sure. Undeterred, the 22 years old started training almost immediately. He was famously pictured hitting tennis balls sitting in a special chair, with his left leg in a cast. Six months later, he returned and went on to be named the ATP's Comeback Player of the Year. The greatest Austrian player in tennis history went onto win 45 titles, including 1995 Roland Garros French Open Grand Slam title.

In 1996, he was ranked World No. 1 in tennis.

Thomas Muster went on to win a lot more titles on major clay court (Ref B. 8, B. 9) Tennis Tournaments around the world. He lifted seven trophies and won 55 of his 65 matches on red clay surface. Two years later, he was crowned the "King of Clay" when he won 40 consecutive clay-court matches.

Thomas Muster played his last professional match in May 1999, moved to Queensland, Australia, lost his fitness and bloated in weight. However, the great Austrian Sportsman never made a formal retirement announcement, but he made occasional appearances on the ATP Champions Tour and was his nation's Davis Cup captain. He enjoyed playing tennis as ever.

After 11 years he staged a comeback. After undergoing a punishing fitness regime, working out for up to seven hours a day, he brought his weight down to the same level he had weighed at the age of 22 (Ref B.8, B.9) and a vastly improved game. He showed the world that he was still a force to reckon with in the world of tennis. In November 2011 at Vienna, he said farewell to tennis. Thomas Muster continues to play tennis and is useful to his nation and the world as a role model sportsmans to emulate.

The moral of this real time story is that to live life well, we need to look at our distant dreams, but we need to live each year, each month and each day well with joy and vigour, believing in the cosmic energy around us which is propelling us to think and act every single moment of our lives in a positive way.

Stay Motivated– From Now Till the End

Motivation is about living with a dream for the future taking steps one day at a time, crossing each mile stone or goal on the way, enjoying the journey with drive and enthusiasm. The dream or vision post will come to pass as did the goal posts and the mile stones. New dreams and goals will emerge. The choice is to leave the past and learn from it, live the now well, plan and live the future equally well as it comes along till you have no more goals to cross except surrender completely at the merciful, kind feet of the God almighty, when you think the judgement day has arrived.

The Purpose of the Book.

I intend to share with the reader all that I know about motivation, theories and academic research work done by me and other experts and scholars on motivation. I have a great desire to share with every one, my knowledge on the relevance of motivation in work life and its role in personal life of individuals reading this book. Barriers to motivation is a chapter in which I have distinctly brought about the difference between self-induced blocks and others induced blocks as barriers to human motivation and ways to combat them.

Simple tips to the common man useful in a practical way for daily use have been mentioned by me in a very simple, readable and implementable way in one of the chapters. A lot of the matter pertaining to work life motivation and personal motivation discussed in this book has been the result of my own thinking, research and teaching for over 23 years of my life at the PG level in management in many Colleges and Universities. I have dedicated a separate chapter to managing stress in life and the connection between motivation and stress management. This should very much interest those working people in offices and corporates as well as those women who stay at home and look after domestic responsibilities which can sometimes turn 'mundane', leading to a lack of motivation and dullness in people's lives.

In short, this book is intended to be read by academicians, scholars, college students, corporate, industry and business personnel, government employees and of course, the house wife looking after her 'home', not to mention the 'husband' who lends her support to succeed in that wholesome, noble cause. It is meant for each and every one in India and abroad.

I am sure this book will benefit all to gain deeper knowledge on the phenomenon of motivation. With the knowledge gained, I am sure, one can live life in a happier, purposeful, efficient, effective, fruitful and complete manner. That is the whole purpose. Now, please, read on.

References

Journals, Articles

B.8 Thomas Muster- Wikipedia, the free encyclopaedia *en.wikipedia.org/wiki/Thomas_Muster.*

B.9 Thomas Muster – Tennis Players -Tennis -ATP World Tour *www.atpworldtour.com/Tennis/Players/Mu/T/Thomas-Muster.asp.*

1

Basics of Motivation

'If you have built castles in the air, your work need not be lost; that is where they should be. Now, put foundations under them.'

Henry David Thoreau

'To find what you seek in the road of life, the best proverb of all is that which says: "Leave no stone unturned.'

Edward Bulwer Lytton

Basics of Motivation and Its Importance

The study of human motivation is of great importance in any theory of management. Man is by nature constantly motivated. He is an organic system. The energy he receives from his surroundings through all his senses is converted to equal action resulting in behaviour. His behaviour is also governed by the relationships between him and the environment which consists of people. Management involves creation and maintenance of environment for performance in which people can perform and be productive while they maintain or sustain their motivation levels constantly throughout their stay in the concerned work environment and also in their personal lives.

The Motivation Process (Ref A.7, A. 8)

Motivation is a six phased process which starts with a need deficiency in an individual and his eventual equal need fulfillment.

The six stages involved in the motivational process are:

(1) Need deficiency.

(2) Search for fulfillment of need.

(3) Goal definition and Goal directed behaviour

(4) Evaluation of performance.

(5) Evaluation of rewards and punishments.

(6) Re-evaluation of needs.

Diagrammatically it can be represented by the following model.

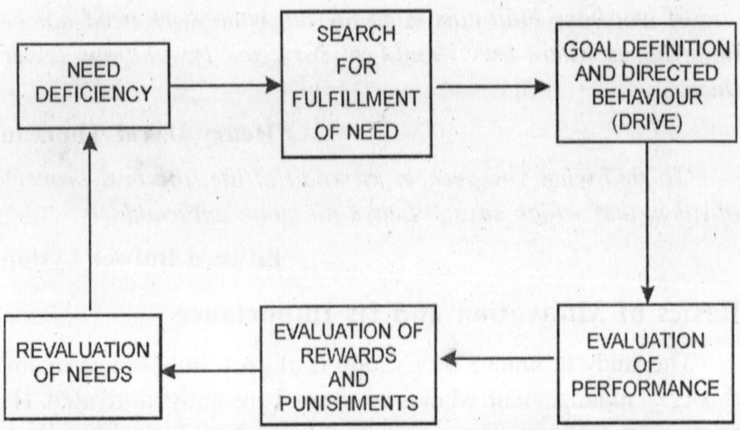

(Fig.1)

When a person has a need for anything unfulfilled (need deficiency), he searches for ways and means (strategy) to fulfill the need and develops a goal directed behaviour (drive). In that process he obtains results which he evaluates (performance) for satisfaction or dissatisfaction (punishments) and reevaluates his needs for more motivation (the cycle repeats).

The entire process described above constitutes motivation. The model is applicable to the personal lives of individuals as well as their work lives.

Before we describe the theories of motivation, let us dwell on equal the definition of motivation for a while.

Definition of Motivation (Ref A. 6, A. 7, A. 8)

Webster defines 'motivate' as to 'provide with a motive,' to 'impel', 'incite' and 'motive' as 'that within the individual, rather than without , which incites him to action; any idea, need emotion or organic state that prompts to an action.'Incite' is also defined as 'to arouse to action, spur or urge on'.

Thus, in order to arouse an individual in to action, it is desirable to determine the motive involved. As this is within the individual, it becomes necessary to study his needs and emotions. It calls definitely for a study of the factors which 'incite' (Incentives) and those which have the opposite effect (Disincentives). Austin defines disincentive as that which impedes or tends to impede determination or action. Some popular definitions of motivation are given below.

Definition 1

'How behaviour gets started, is energised, is sustained, is directed, is stopped, and what kind of subjective reaction is present in the organism while all this is going on' (Jones, 1955).

Definition 2

'Motivation is the result of processes, internal or external to the individual, that arouse enthusiasm and persistence to pursue a certain course of action.'

Definition 3

'Motivation is a process that starts with a physiological or psychological deficiency or need that activates behaviour or a drive that is aimed at a goal or an incentive.'

Out of all the above definitions given, the first one covers all the six stages involved in the motivation process indicated in Fig.1.

Importance of Motivation (Ref B. 1, B. 2)

There are several reasons as to why motivation is vital to an organisational work situation and in the personal life of an individual. The reasons are listed below:

- Motivated people try and do work in ways different from the usual at home and in the work place.
- Motivated people are interested in producing work, which is quality oriented both at home and in a work place.
- Highly motivated people are much more productive than the others. Example: There are several factors attributed to the high levels of productivity in Japan, but motivation is the main factor.
- Every organization requires human resources, in addition to the need for financial and material and other kinds of physical resources. Three behavioural dimensions of human beings are significant to the organisation.
- People must be attracted not only to join an organisation but also must be motivated to stay in it. This implies that an organisation must pay a lot of attention to the motivational environment in a company as well as his personal goals and aspirations.
- The advent of new technology and its impact on production also demands a thorough study of motivation. Example: Operations like the launch of a satellite in to the orbit, carried out by Space Research Organisations call for a great deal of human effort, co-ordination and top of it all motivation to not only to succeed but sustain it as well.
- In the past the organisations had learnt to look at their technical and financial resources. Only recently, they are learning to give a serious thought to the appropriate use of their human resources. Many organisations are learning to look at their employees as their future resources or "Talent Banks". The increasing evidence of this trend is seen in many organisations which are popularising concepts such as "Assessment Center" appraisals, "Human Resource Accounting" etc. More concern is being shown in

implementing ideas such as job enrichment, job rotation, training etc. mainly in order to motivate employees so that they become more productive.

The next chapter, no 2, introduces the reader to some of the popular, contemporary theories on motivation. The author believes that even a knowledgeable academician or a researcher, leave alone the common man, need to brush up his fundamentals on motivation by reading the contents of this chapter before he begins to appreciate the value of what is offered in the succeeding chapters from 3 onwards.

References

Books

A.6. Keith Davis and J.W.Newstrom, "Human Behaviour at Work-Organizational Behaviour", Mcgraw-Hill, Newyork,1989.

A.7. Fred Luthens, "Organizational Behaviour", Mcgraw- Hill Inc., Newyork,1995.

A.8. Dr. Anjali Ghanekar, "Organizational Behaviour, Concepts and Cases", Everest Publishing House, Pune, Eighth Edition, 2002.

Journals, Articles

B.1. David C.Mclellend, "Managing Motivation to Expand Human Freedom", American Psychologist, 1978.

B.2. Dr Viswanathan Gopalan, "Motivation and Its Relevance to Productivity". Thesis for Ph.D, Pune University, 2001.

2

Critical Ideas, Terms, Meanings and Concepts in Motivation

'You are never too old to set another goal or to dream a new dream.'

C. S. Lewis

'The will to win, the desire to succeed, the urge to reach your full potential... these are the keys that will unlock the door to personal excellence'.

Confucius

Introduction

Before we get in to the issue of understanding some of the theories on motivation which explain human needs and behaviour, it is essential for the reader, especially the newcomer or the novice and even the academician, the researcher or a student pursuing higher education to appreciate and understand the deeper meanings of the terms used in the motivational paradigm and the concepts there of. The following paragraphs deal with all those terms and concepts. The author has tried to make the explanations as simple as possible so that the reader can enjoy reading and grasping these very fundamental basics which are absolutely critical to assimilate what comes as knowledge in the next chapters on motivation.

The Difference between 'Motive' and 'Motivation'

'Motive' can be defined as 'An inner urge that activates, propels or moves the individual towards a 'goal' directed behaviour'. We will explain the meanings of the terms 'behaviour' and goal shortly. Before that, let us go deeper in to the explanation the above definition offers.

Some authors distinguish between the words 'needs' and 'motives' I believe that they can be used interchangeably. The only point I need to mention here is that 'motive' can be a collection of a number of critical needs or can be one dominant single need however, it is generally a combination of critical needs unsatisfied and need satisfaction either consciously or sub-consciously.

The term 'motivation' on he other hand implies the entire process consisting of need, drive, behaviour, goal attainment, feedback regarding success of goal achievement and continuation of the cycle of motivation. Motive is only a part of motivation but critical to motivation. It is very important and essential.

Motives can be classified in to three types.

1. *Primary Motives* – These are physical needs such as hunger, thirst, the need to sleep, sex and so on. These are not learned, but are present physiologically in the individual right from birth.
2. *General Motives* – These are also not learned but are present in individuals as psychological needs such as curiosity, competence, affection, manipulation and so on.
3. *Secondary Motives* – These are learned by the individual during the process of his growth and interaction with society. The need for affiliation, achievement, power, status etc. is learned motives which are prevalent among human beings both in personal lives as well as in their career lives. These motives need to be fulfilled by organisations when they try and motivate employees for greater performance.

These secondary motives are socio-psychological. They are not directly related to survival motives like hunger or thirst. They are learned in a social organisation of any kind. They can further be classified in to :

1. Affirmative motive and
2. Egoistic motives.

Affirmative motives are positive such as friendliness, kindness, helpfulness, the need to work as a team and so on. Egoistic needs are 'power-cetered' such as the need to 'control' others, 'status', money, position and so on. Both these types of motives operate in work environments in deciding the motivation levels of people and hence are very important in studies on motivation.

Behaviour

Behaviour stems from motives. Behaviour is action from motives directed at a 'goal'. The behaviour of an individual may be driven 'consciously' by the individual or sometimes 'subconsciously'. An example may be when an author says he writes a book for contribution as knowledge to society consciously, he may be subconsciously working for name, fame and money. The motives and the goals may vary from individual to individual in a given situation which may appear same or similar which makes motivation a complex phenomenon.

However, it is important for individuals to reflect, understand their conscious and subconscious motives through quiet reflection while pursuing goals or objectives which will fulfil those needs or motives. Otherwise, situations may arise in which the individual turns back and asks the question, "Why did I do it?" or "Why did I not think of it in advance?"

Goals

Goals are specific, outside the individual and achievable. These may be called as 'incentives' by psychologists to motivate the individual. A goal in a work situation may be something as clear as pay, a promotion, a perk like a bonus or a status symbol such as a car, a cabin etc. In personal lives goal can be things clearly achievable like a house, a car, a bank balance, a good ward robe full of dresses and so on. When we analyse life's issues in the motivational paradigm, it is important to distinguish clearly between needs or motives and goals. Sometimes the individual begins to mix up both. He may think that the need or the motive is what he is seeking. He should set goals clearly and drive himself to reach the goals thus satisfying the needs or motives which drove him to do so.

From now on we will use the term 'need' interchangeably with 'motive' in the rest of the chapters for the sake of simplicity.

Some of the complexities and challenges in the motivational model of human behaviour.

We have understood from the foregoing discussions that 'motivation' is all about identification of one's own needs or motives, setting a goal to achieve and indulge in a behaviour with drive so that the goal can be reached or attained. The model can become a little complex or difficult to understand when the following difficulties arise.

1. The needs or motives in different individuals may be the same but the goals can be totally different. For example, two individual want to achieve fame and money. One may decide to become a sportsman while another chooses to write a book, while a third guy decides to become an actor. The choices and motives are left to the individuals and the reasons are sometimes not clear to the individuals.
2. The need and goal are clear to an individual but the paths to achieve and hence the behavioural options are many and so the individual may face conflicts in selection. As an example, let us say an individual wants to contribute to society through social work. He may have choices like one, serve the old and the elderly, two, serve the children who are orphaned or three, work for the visually handicapped and young. Deciding on a final option and developing a 'commitment' to do so may call for a lot of reflection and intra-personal conflict resolution by the individual.
3. Some motives may be clear and conscious while some may be in the subconscious and may not be understood clearly

by the individual. Example, a book writer thinks he is contributing through knowledge to society while subconsciously he may be working for fame and money too.

4. As discussed earlier, motives may vary from culture to culture for similar goals. Goals may be different from culture to culture for similar motives.
5. A combination of needs in varying degrees of strength may constitute the motives for achieving a goal. The most dominant of these needs may decide the final outcome.

Conclusion

All said and done, the reader is encouraged to think that if he has understood the basic concepts, ideas and terms used to explain the phenomenon of motivation, he should have no difficulty in comprehending what the future chapters of this book have to offer to him in terms of knowledge and wisdom.

References

Books

A.7. Fred Luthens, "Organisational Behaviour," Mcgraw- Hill Inc., Newyork, 1995.

A.8. Dr. Anjali Ghanekar, "Organizational Behaviour, Concepts and Cases," Everest Publishing House, Pune, Eighth Edition, 2002.

Journals

B. 1. David C.Mclellend, "Managing Motivation to Expand Human Freedom," American Psychologist, 1978.

B. 2. Dr.Viswanathan Gopalan, "Motivation and Its Relevance to Productivity." Thesis for Ph.D, Pune University, 2001.

3

Theories of Motivation

'If you can imagine it, you can achieve it; if you can dream it, you can become it.'

William Arthur Ward

'If you would create something, you must be something.'

Johann Wolfgang Von Goethe

There are several approaches to the study of human motivation and especially motivation in a work place. Broadly speaking, there are two kinds of theories related to work behaviour and motivation in work environments. They are:

1. The early Theories:

(a) Scientific Management by F.W. Taylor

(b) Human Relations Model by Elton Mayo

2. Contemporary Theories:

(a) Maslow's Need Hierarchy Theory

(b) Herzberg's Two Factor Theory

(c) Alderfer's ERG Theory

(d) Mcclelland's 3N Theory (3 needs)

(e) Manifest Needs Theory

(f) Vroom's Expectancy Model

(g) Adam's Equity Theory

(h) Porter's Performance Satisfaction Theory

The early theories evolved when industrialization was just beginning to happen on this planet in a big way. Times have changed and a lot has happened. Today we are in an era of high-tech on the fast lane. Hence, I did not wish to talk about the validity of those theories in this book.

Instead, I chose the following "Content" theories, content implying the "Human Need Factor" as the basis for our discussion and the knowledge of the reader. These are the most significant according to me. I sincerely believe and my lifetime involvement I research on 'Human Motivation' confirm my belief that the need classifications defined and structured by these theories are very much relevant and applicable in the personal lives of individuals also. We are going to discuss and understand three of the most relevant of the contemporary content theories which are mentioned below:

(a) Maslow's Need Hierarchy Theory

(b) Herzberg's Two Factor Theory

(c) Mcclelland's 3N (Achievement, Affiliation, Power) need theory.

A detailed description of the above follows. A word of caution however. It would have been impossible to cover the relevance of all theories because the field is too vast and exhaustive to engage in such a kind of investigation and I am sure very little will come out of it. I have, however, for the sake of completion, mentioned very briefly, at the end of the chapter, the significance of some contemporary 'cognitive' theories like:

(d) Adam's Equity Theory

(e) Vroom's Expectancy Model

Porter-Lawler's Performance Satisfaction Theory, which is also cognitive in nature and its relevance in human motivation has been separately discussed in the chapter 6 on the 'Connection between motivation and performance in work places'. To begin with, let us look at some of the 'Content' theories in greater detail.

Content Theories

These theories use individual needs to help in the understanding of job satisfaction and work behaviours. Needs reflect physiological or psychological deficiencies. Content theories agree that stated more clearly content theorists suggest that in order to motivate people, their needs must be assessed and the rewards decided .

Need ⟶ Activate ⟶ Tensions ⟶ That influence ⟶ Work Behavior

Maslow's Need Hierarchy Theory (Ref A. 1, A. 8, B. 2)

Abraham Harold Maslow is the proponent of his famous theory on motivation based on a "Hierarchy of needs." It is by far the simplest and the best known of all theories on motivation. The essence of the theory can be summarised as follows:

- People are wanting beings whose unsatisfied needs influence their behaviour. The satisfied needs do not motivate while the unsatisfied does.
- There are a number of needs a human being has to cope with and they are arranged in an order of importance (hierarchy) from basic to the most complex.
- A human being advances from one from one need to another from his basic needs to the more complex, but only when the lower level need of his is fully satisfied.
- As a human being moves further up in his hierarchy of needs, he will display more humanness and psychological maturity and health and will move towards happiness and joy.

The needs : According to Maslow, human needs are grouped into five levels of which the basic level of need comprises of the primary or the physiological ones. The model is illustrated in Fig. 2.

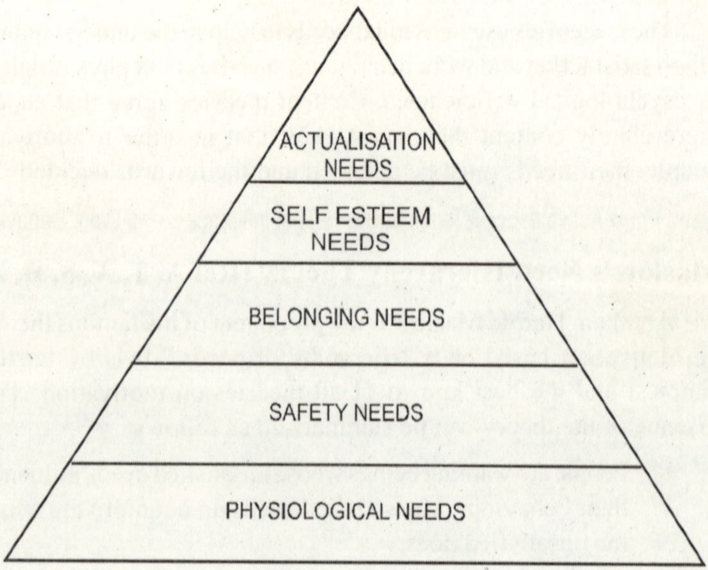

Fig.2

Physiological Needs

This is the most basic of all the human needs and the most powerful. Included in this category are needs like the desire for food, thirst, sex, sleep etc., satisfying these needs are absolutely essential for the human organism to survive. In other words, the human being will not be around and may perish if these needs are not satisfied for a long period.

Maslow States

For our chronically, extremely, hungry man, Utopia can be simply defined as a place where there is plenty of food. He tends to think that if only he is guaranteed food for the rest of his life, he will probably be happy and will never want anything more.Life itself is defined in terms of eating. Anything else will be defined as unimportant. Freedom, love, community feeling, respect, philosophy may all be waved aside as fripperies that are useless, since they fail to fill the stomach. Such a man may fairly said to live by bread alone (1970)

Security or Safety Needs

Next to the physical needs in the order of priority is the security or the safety need of the person which in essence is equal more psychological than physical. We deal with factors such as the absence of fear of losing a job and livelihood, fear of living safely and comfortably etc.

Safety needs play a dominant role in a person's life right from childhood. As a person becomes an adult, the needs still dominate. The desire to have a good education, have a secured job with a secured income, the need to have a home with a supportive family etc., are part of this continuing need to have security in life.

From an organisational point of view, the security needs could include factors such as job security, safe working conditions, long term benefits such as pension, provident fund, gratuity, pay revisions to cope with inflationary tendencies in the market, health schemes for the employees and family etc.

Belongingness and Love Need

This constitutes the third level of security in Maslow's hierarchy of needs. The individual affected by this need, longs to be part of a group either in his family or work place. He strives for acceptance in to a group either formal or informal. Group membership becomes a dominant goal for the individual. Accordingly, the person may feel the pangs of loneliness or the bliss of 'company'.

Sigmund Freud believed that love meant "Sex" while Maslow said there can be a healthy relationship between two individuals based on mutual trust and affection and love not involving necessarily sex. Maslow was emphatic that the need involves both giving and receiving. Not being loved leads to a feeling of emptiness, hostility and futility.

In the organisational context, this need can exemplify compatible work groups, peer acceptance, professional friendship and friendly supervision.

Self-esteem Needs

Once the individual satisfies his belonging needs, according to Maslow, he tries to address his self-esteem needs. Maslow has classified these needs in to two further subsets:

1. self –respect and
2. respect from others.

Self-respect can imply feelings such as confidence, competence, personal strength, adequacy, achievement, independence and freedom. An individual has the right to know that he, as a human being is worthwhile, is capable of contributing and at the same time capable of mastering skills which will enable him to succeed. Esteem from others may include factors such as prestige, recognition, attention, acceptance, status, reputation and appreciation. In this case the individual experience feelings of worth because the others recognize him.

Satisfaction of the self-esteem needs generates feelings and attitudes of self-confidence, usefulness and self-worth, being at harmony with the world. In case these needs are not met with, the individual may feel futile, worthless and hence may feel frustrated and dejected.

The danger of the esteem needs in an individual is that he may begin to rely on others to pass a judgment about his worth exclusively and hence may become very dependent. Others can control him and victimize him in to a position of dependency and lack of confidence. In order not to fall a prey to this 'victim' process, the individual has to focus on one's own approval and worth than others worth and others approval.

In a work environment self-esteem needs may correspond to job titles, recognition by others, challenging work, responsibility etc. Managerial practices which can fulfill these needs may include providing employees with challenging work assignments, job enrichment, positive feed backs on good performance, adding skills through training, recognition through appropriate reward systems, providing a caring, nurturing environment, allowing employees to participate in decision making and so on.

Self-actualisation Needs:

This indicates, according to maslow, the desire of the human being to realise one's full potential with regard to certain needs. This can be just as simple as doing work for the sheer joy of it and excelling in it without so much caring about others approval and recognition and focusing so much more on inner satisfaction. People who work at this level have a very high esteem for themselves. They are driven by a "PURPOSE" which is larger than life itself.

Though the need to be self-fulfilled seems very necessary, only a few, the so called "Enlightened" seem to realise it. Maslow himself has estimated that less than one persent of the population fulfills the need for self-actualisation in the entire world.

Maslow Advances Three Reasons for This Happening:

1. People are really not "Aware" of their own potentials.
2. Social environment often stifles the development of an individual.
3. The most important bottleneck to growth and fulfillment may be the need to be safe. The human being may regress periodically from growing because he may not be willing to take risks. Growing is all about taking risks and the desire to learn.

In an organisational set up, self-actualisation need may manifest in an individual in his need to excel in jobs, the need to come out with ideas and be creative, the desire to create something new which nobody has done before and so on. Managers who encourage people to be creative are specifically enhancing the self-actualisation needs in individuals. Changing, growing organisations must address this need in individuals if they want to benefit from the excellence of a few individuals.

Deficit vs Growth Motivation

Maslow also distinguishes between "Deficiency" and "Growth" needs. Deficiency needs correspond to physical and security needs approximately. Deficiency or D-needs in an individual imply that if the need is there like starving or dying of thirst, the organism can not "focus" on anything else. Maslow meant by growth needs, the desire to attain happiness which implies the higher level need from belonging to self-actualisation.

Growth needs or Meta needs or B-motives indicate a person's urge to bring out his in born potentials. Growth needs are not concerned about "tension" reductions as about expansion of mental horizons in order to achieve one's own inner potentials in life.

The Merits and Limitations of the Need Hierarchy Model

First, Maslow's Need Hierarchy theory is by far the most popular of all motivational theories. In fact, we can safely say that there is no one, no manager in an organisation who is not familiar with this theory. Every one identifies himself or herself with this theory that it is easy to recognize these needs in individuals and the organisation can try and satisfy these needs so that the individual fees motivated and so the organisation can hope for more output (productivity) from the individual.

Secondly, Maslow seems to answer questions which have puzzled managers and other individuals in a work place. Sometimes, the management wonders why certain individuals are motivated by money while a few do not care. Maslow's need hierarchy theory supplies the answers for the intra and inter personal variations in behaviour in a given situation in a work place.

Thirdly, Maslow's need model describes human needs and behaviour as a very dynamic activity expressing itself as a constant desire to change for better growth through the process of attainment of unfulfilled higher level needs. The theory states that man or woman does not rest on past glories but moves on restlessly until his or her actualisation potentials are fulfilled which may never be the case in many individuals and hence the world remains an active place.

Fourthly, Maslow was the one to deviate from the early theories on human behaviour proposed by colossals in the field of psychology such as Freud who believed all behaviour is the result of the sexual needs in individuals. Maslow's beliefs are based on EXISTENTIAL PHILOSOPHY which states that man is a very creative being, different from animals, striving constantly to lead a meaningful life of achievement and finally reach his destined full potential. Maslow must be credited for the positive psychology he introduced in behaviour analysis and modification and hence contributing immensely to the study of motivation.

Lastly, the theory is extremely simple and easy to understand. It is excellent because of its humanness and intuitiveness.

There are several criticisms and limitations to the theory.

1. First and foremost, the hierarchy which Maslow talks about does not exist in practice. All the need of human beings are parallely existing, some dominant and others not so dominant. Another criticism against Maslow's theory is that even if the needs in human beings are hierarchical in order, the need priorities may vary from culture to culture and hence perhaps from country to country. For example in India, the basic or the physiological needs may be at the bottom of the scale while in a country like America, it may be at the middle of the pyramid of needs. In a country like Japan, social needs may be at the highest level and so on.
2. The same argument may be applicable to differing types of organisational cultures. In a country like India, there are various kinds of organisations like the public sectors, the private sectors, and among the private sector enterprises those run by family controlled organisations like those belonging to some communities, those belonging to some of the affluent families and so on. The need pattern in individuals "Adjusted" to the above cultures may be different in these situations.

In spite of all the limitations and criticisms mounted against it Maslow's theory explains best the importance of human needs in a work situation, especially the significance of higher order needs like esteem and actualisation. I strongly felt that even in the current changing scenario in the world of Internetworking and global advance in technology, Maslow's need model can explain why people may decide to produce or refrain from it.

Herzberg's Two Factor Theory (Motivation-Hygiene Theory) (Ref A. 4,A. 8)

This model was introduced by Herzberg and his associates in mid –50s. called in a variety of ways such as the two factor theory or the dual factor theory or the motivation hygiene theory. The theory distinguishes between job content factors or satisfiers such as achievement, recognition, the work itself, responsibility, advancement, growth opportunities etc., and the job context factors or dissatisfiers such as company policy and administration, supervision, working condition, environment, safety, security and other similar factors.

The satisfiers were also called motivators. Herzberg said that the dissatisfiers when working effectively did not motivate employees but if they were not taken care of, contributed to dissatisfaction or de-motivation. On the other hand, Herzberg felt that the satisfiers or motivators did make a direct contribution to motivation.

According to Herzberg, satisfaction and dissatisfaction are not opposite poles in one dimension but they are two independent dimensions. Satisfaction is affected by motivators and dissatisfaction by hygiene factors. To achieve motivation in a work environment, the hygiene factors are to be ensured removing dissatisfaction and the satisfiers are to be provided ensuring motivation and hence satisfaction to the people involved in activities.

Explains the gist of the two-factor theory in a diagrammatic manner.

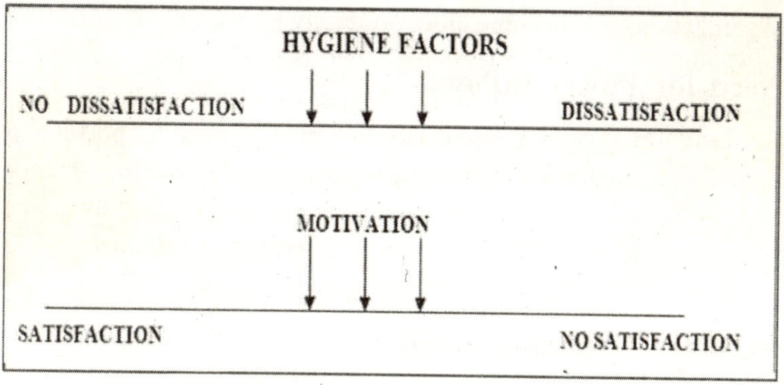

Fig. 3

The hygiene factors are equivalent to the physiological, security and social needs in Maslow's need hierarchy model while the higher level needs in Maslow's pyramid corresponds to the motivators in Herzberg's two factor theory of motivation.

The 3 N theory of Achievement, Affiliation and Power by David C. McClelland (Ref A. 2, A. 8, B. 1)

David C. Mc Chell and C. Mclell name and his associates, in 1940, proposed this theory on human motivation which is popularly called the 3n theory, emphasizes primarily on the needs of high achievers (nach) in work places. However, Chell name studied the power (nPow) as well as the affiliation (nAff) of individuals in organisations. Briefly stated the theory is as follows.

Need for Achievement (nAch)

There are high achievers in work places who achieve tasks quickly and assess themselves for performance and satisfaction. They earn a lot of wealth not for the sake of money per sent but with a view to measure themselves with wealth as a yard stick.

These persons take moderate and not high levels of risk. They like tasks of reasonable difficulties and dislike easy tasks and easy success. They work independently and like to achieve independently.

McClellend believed that these high achievers can be made role models in industries for others to emulate so that the organizations can become more productive.

Need for Power (nPow)

Individuals exist in organisations with high need for power and they derive satisfaction from being in positions of power to influence and control others. Organisations, which encourage an authoritative environment, attract individuals with power need and they tend to perform better than others in those places.

Need for Affiliation (nAff)

An organisation consists of individuals of this category, who are motivated to have a strong bondage with others for interpersonal ties and to get close to them psychologically. Persons with high affiliation needs tend to choose friends than competent persons in order to work in groups.

As mentioned earlier, I have very briefly mentioned, the following 'cognitive' theories on motivation, for the sake of providing full awareness to the reader on the subject.

Cognitive or Process Theories of Motivation (Ref A. 8)

Cognitive Theories are based on the concept that people in work places make conscious decisions on job behaviour. Managements wanting to motivate these employees must understand these cognitions and behaviour patterns in individuals.

Adam's Equity Theory (Ref A. 8)

This theory was proposed, in 1965, by James Stacy Adams. The theory is based on his belief that human beings in work places perform well if they are treated with 'Equity' in relation to others. Adams said that this term 'Equity' represents an equation which ensures that:

$$\frac{\text{Output of Self}}{\text{Inputs given to self}} = \frac{\text{Output of Others}}{\text{Inputs given to others}}$$

In other words, he constantly modifies his behaviour to perform in such a manner that if he is given less. He will perform less in comparison to those around and he will perform more if given more than those around.

The main point that the equity theory emphasizes is that the individual in a work place uses his 'perceived notion' of being treated on par with everyone in an to behave and perform. The negativeness of the theory is that these perceptions of equity of individuals is difficult to understand and measure and hence the theory is not practical and complex

Vroom's Expectancy Theory (Ref A. 8)

Victor H Vroom, in the year 1964, proposed that human beings in work environments performed based on their expectancies which are:

1. Increased effort will lead to increased performance.
2. Increased performance will lead to increased rewards.

He also said that -

The 'Valence or Strength of the desire to perform The Expectancy or the Probability of Success. The strength or the Valence of motivation' in a mathematical equation of the model.

Vroom's expectancy theory emphasises the idea that in work places the employees expect that hard work will result in improved reward situations. This is something the managements have to appreciate. The content theories simplify human behaviour in terms of needs while the cognitive expectancy theory of Vroom brings in unknown factors like expectations of individuals in to picture in the overall gamut of motivation. This theory is of practical significance in understanding human behaviour vis a vis motivation in work places.

Conclusion

I wish to conclude this chapter by sharing with the reader of this book the thought that individuals in today's organisations and in personal life are driven by these expectancies, motives and needs equal in order to perform and stay motivated. The theories discussed above form the basis for connecting to the concept of motivation and look at it in the right perspective. Finally I plan to convince the reader in the remaining portions of the book as to how motivation contributes to the happiness and well being in people in their professional and personal lives.

References

Books

A. 1. AH. Maslow, "Motivationand Personality", Harper & Bros, Newyork, 1054.

A. 2. D. C. Mclellend, "The Achieving", D. Nostrandco. Inc, Princeton, N.J.,1961

A. 4.Frederick, "Hertzberg, Bernard" Mausner and Barbara Shydermann, "The Motivation to Work", 2nd Edition, John Wiley and Son. Inc, Newyork, 1959.

A. 8. Dr Anjali Ghanekar, "Organizational Behaviour, Concepts and Cases," Everest Publishing House, Pune, Eighth Edition, 2002.

Journals, Articles

B. 1. David C.Mclellend, "Managing Motivation to expand Human Freedom," American Psychologist,1978.

B. 2. Dr. Viswanathan Gopalan, "Motivation and Its Relevance to Productivity." Thesis for Ph.D, Pune University, 2001.

4

Barriers to Motivation

'First they ignore you, then they laugh at you, then they fight you, then you win.'

Mahatma Gandhi

'Success is not measured by the heights one attains, but by the obstacles one overcomes in its attainment.'

Booker T. Washington

In this chapter, we will introduce to the reader some of the common obstacles and challenges faced by people in a work environment or in personal life which will result in loss of motivation and hence lead to frustration and lack of performance. We are going to show how these obstacles or 'barriers' to motivation can be dealt with and overcome.

The Frustration Model of Motivation (Ref A. 8, B. 1, B. 2)

We have understood from the foregoing chapters that motivation consists of a process involving need identification ——a Drive——a Goal achievement.

Imagine an obstacle or a barrier being introduced between the drive and the goal portion of this process. What occurs as a result is a phenomenon called frustration for the individual involved I the motivational issue.

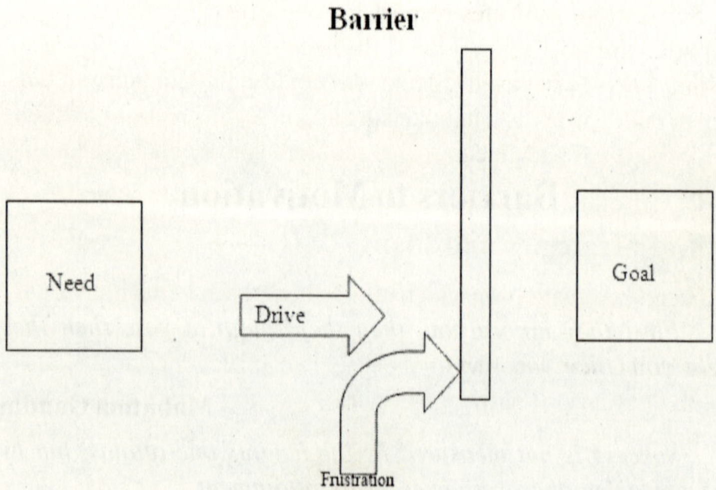

Fig. 4

Frustration

Frustration can occur because of the barrier which can be physical like someone physically pulling you away from reaching your goals or psychological of your own making or imposed by those around. We will be focusing in the following paragraphs, on the psychological and socio-psychological barriers detrimental to motivation and some of the means or techniques we can adopt in order to face them, overcome them and stay motivated to reach the set goal.

Psychological,Self-induced Barriers Self-Doubts

These can range from uncertainty of understanding the needs, lack of clarity regarding goals, losing drive when difficulties are encountered on the way to achieving a goal, uncertainty regarding one's own ability to sustain the drive and reach the goal and so on.

Lack of Self-esteem

Self-esteem indicates respect for oneself regardless of what others think of you. Even if the skills to achieve a goal or vision is missing, a person with self-esteem will not lose faith in himself, but go on to build the skills without losing heart. So, motivation calls for a lot of self-esteem needs to be satisfied and dealt with in an individual.

Lack of Strategies and Plans

There are situations in which the needs are clear to the individual and so are the goals and the guy has enough energy and drive. However, he may lack the knowledge and skills to strategize and plan the process of moving forward that after a while he loses direction and control. The net result is the loss of energy and purpose. Despite efforts, the end of the tunnel does not seem to be visible.

Lack of a Long-Term Dream or Vision

Some people identify needs; work on short term goals with drive and enthusiasm. However, they are unable to dream big and sustain the dream for long periods of time. This results in their spending efforts at doing several short term projects successfully, but they are unable to stay focused on certain long term, self-discovering initiatives which can give them prolonged happiness and satisfaction. In other words, these people are hard workers and achievers, but lack direction and purpose in life and career.

Social Barriers to Motivation (Ref A. 8, B. 1, B. 2)

In many instances, the individual has clear cut needs, sufficient drive and long term goals defined, but lacks social support, approval and sanctions to carryout the tasks leading to fulfilment of needs and achievement of dreams. The following are some of those issues which the individual needs to be aware of so that he can tide over them wherever they are missing and not feel demotivated and frustrated.

Others do not Approve–Approval or Power Need

If you are working for satisfying the needs or sometimes the egos of other people and they do not give that final nod of approval of what you are doing or about to do, there is every possibility that you end up in frustration.

Others do not Delegate Responsibility and Authority-Power Need

In several situations, you are reporting in a structure of hierarchy wherein the people above need to trust you and delegate responsibility commensurate with authority to carryout tasks. The example can be that of a purchase manager in a factory, who is asked to identify a potential supplier of a commodity but not allowed to place an order on the supplier and requires a sanction from his superiors. Another example is that of a housewife who has to take the consent of her earning husband even for the daily purchase of essential goods the household requires. The result of this lack of delegation of power leads to frustration of the individual affected and the consequent demotivation.

Others do not Consult You – Affiliation Need

You are asked to do and shoulder some responsibility, but others above decide what has to be done or how it has to be done and you are told to do the same without questioning the authority of those who told you to do, can be a very frustrating and annoying situation. This is typical scenario in many work situations and this is a great contributor of all-round frustration of individuals and a cause for demotivation and loss of collective morale. This is a dictatorial way of managing things and a leadership style, according to me, which prevails in many places in many organisations. We need to be aware that such a situation can confront us in any work environment or in our personal life situations too.

Others do not Recognise You - Recognition Need

Others know that you have handled responsibility and have

carried out the job well, but still refuse to recognise you, not even give a smile or better still the proverbial pat on the back.

They do not praise you in public in front of others nor give you a certification of merit, none whatsoever. The result can be very devastating for you if you do not know how to handle such a situation in work life.

In personal life, an unappreciative husband can kill the enthusiasm of a housewife or a nagging housewife can do it to a loving, caring husband, either way.

Others do not include and respect you- belonging and esteem needs

An environment in which you do not get the respect you deserve as a person with his or her own views and opinions or a place which treats you as alien can really upset you and make you lose all your motivation to be useful and purposeful. People above you, below you or parallel to you in a hierarchical structure in a company may sometimes treat you with disrespect and contempt that you can end up in a pile of self-pity and frustration. In personal life the same hing can happen in family relationships which can lead to quarrels and resulting break in relationships. Family courts in India are loaded with divorce cases where the main cause of the conflicts has been lack of mutual respect between couples.

Others prevent you from achieving- Achievement Need

This is different from others not encouraging you or recognising you for your efforts. This is a situation in which obstacles physical and psychological are put in front of you by your enemies or detractors so that you are incapacitated from fulfilling your missions or objectives. The only way to tackle this situation is to confront your detractors and bring them to books or punish them through the process of law in case they resort to illegal means of preventing you from exercising your democratic free rights as an individual.

Summary

I have tried to share with the reader, in the foregoing paragraphs some of the main barriers to motivation. Self-induced barriers like self-doubts, lack of self-esteem, lack of strategies and plans, lack of drive and vision are some of the hurdles while social barriers like approval and recognition by others, lack of authority and responsibility to fulfill aspirations in situations where one is dependent on others are factors affecting motivation. In extreme cases, one may have to fight battles to remove obstacles deliberately introduced by others to prevent you from achieving your goals, missions and dreams or visions in life. The key is to think positive, stay positive and motivated in all circumstances and say no to any barrier which comes in the way of staying happy and motivated while you continue to make progress in achieving your life's missions.

References

Books

A. 8. Dr. Anjali Ghanekar, "Organisational Behaviour, Concepts and Cases," Everest Publishing House, Pune, Eighth Edition, 2002.

Journals, Articles

B. 1. David C.Mclellend, "Managing Motivation to expand Human Freedom," American Psychologist,1978.

B. 2. Dr.Viswanathan Gopalan, "Motivation and Its Relevance to Productivity".Thesis for Ph.D Pune University, 2001.

5

Motivation in Personal Life

'No great man ever complains of want of opportunities.'

Ralph Waldo Emerson

'Happy are those who dream dreams and are ready to pay the price to make them come true.'

Leon J. Suenes

In this chapter, I wish to share with the reader some of the most important tips regarding making motivation work for every individual on a daily basis, but also will result in the achievement of his or her long term goals and visions as well.

Going back to the models on motivation which I described for the reader in the earlier chapters, I would say three elements stand out distinctly in the realisation and achievement of motivation in any one's life. They are:

1. Identification of one's inner needs
2. Setting up a goal to achieve the result.
3. Developing a plan and maintaining a 'Drive' during the process.

We are going to discuss these three processes in detail in the following pages.

Identifying one's Own Inner Needs

In fact, while a person develops a desire to do or achieve

anything, in many cases, he is unable to understand what drives him to do so. He is unable to connect his yearning for a specific object of desire to the core of a burning need in him. This is one of the reasons which prevents people from sustaining the desire when the obstacles come and frustration sets in.

Many people react when asked the question, "Why do you do it?" with an immediately answer, "Money". They do not realise that money is not a need, but a means of transacting values. We require money to buy an object like a house or a car. We, in that instance, are addressing our need to buy a house or a car, which could be a physical security need or a status need to be accepted as an important person in society. It can be the esteem and worth need of an individual and in some cases, buying the house may be the ultimate dream or vision of a person in life in which case it tends towards actualisation. Without making this discussion complicated, I wish to point out that while developing ambitions to achieve, one should become need aware.

When an athlete achieves a medal in the Olympics, he/she could be doing for the honor of the country or merely for the sake of enhancing one's own reputation or both in which case the needs of actualization and self-esteem combined in that individual in the process of achieving the medal and the honors that go with it.

To be brief, the first step in the motivational issues in individual aspirations for achievement is identifying the inner need of an individual, which causes the drive to take place. One should be able to pin point the need clearly as one that belongs to the variety of needs discussed in the various theories on motivation, see, identify and internalise.

Goal Setting

Having identified one's own needs, the next step is to set a clear goal or a set of goals for achievement of an objective. This is like saying, "I am thirsty" or my need is "Thirst" and so my goal is to drink "Water". Then you run around for water, find it, drink it with happiness, quench your thirst and end up satisfied till the thirst occurs again.

The most important considerations in setting goals are:

1. Goals must be specific and achievable.
2. Goals can be achieved within set time limits.
3. Goals must be real and not illusory.

In the example of one drinking water, water can be replaced by other liquids like a fruit juice or coconut water, but cannot be replaced by a harmful acid which may enhance the thirst and simultaneously ruin the liver. Time limits are preferable, else, people may tend to procrastinate and not achieve ever. Some of the searches for a specific goal such as a "Good Guru" or "A true friend" may take longer durations of time than one plans for.

When I say goals must be realistic and not illusory, I mean you cannot set goals like "I want to be the ruler of the world." Set a goal like "I need to be the governor of this district" which is specific and achievable.

Developing a Plan and Sustaining a Drive

The final important step in the motivational process is to develop a strategy or a long term plan to achieve the mission and break it in to achievable short term objectives or goals and set the action plans on from day one. Slowly but steadily the advance begins and the goals are reached and passed by till the final one arrives which will also eventually come to pass. But the point is that the dream, the vision or the mission gets fulfilled yielding satisfaction and happiness to the individual concerned, leaving him more motivated to achieve other dreams in future.

The biggest challenge in the above process is ofcourse the possibility of 'losing the drive' on the way. It is quite possible the path is filled with blocks to the objective of reaching the goal and frustrations occur as a result. One can 'backslide' and reach a point where progress becomes a lot more difficult. On those occasions, one has to muster courage, sustain drive and motivation and move on steadily till the final goal is reached. It is all part of the 'big challenge'.

The following are some tips which will enable the common person to practice motivation easily on a daily basis.

Seven Simple Rules of Staying Motivated

1. Set a major goal, but follows a path

The path has mini goals that go in many directions. When you learn to succeed in achieving mini goals, you will be motivated to challenge grand goals which will lead you to the ultimate goal in your vision.

2. Finish what you start

A half-finished project is of no use to anyone. Quitting is a habit. Develop the habit of finishing self-motivated projects. Perseverance and patience are traits that one must cultivate in order to succeed.

3. Socialise with others of similar interests

Mutual support is motivating. We will develop the attitudes of our best friends. If they are losers, we will be a looser. If they are winners, we will be a winner. So choosing the right friends who have positive attitudes towards life in general is a quality one must develop in order to stay motivated and succeed in doing things.

4. Learn how to learn

Dependency on others for knowledge is a slow time consuming processes. Man has the ability to learn without instructors. In fact, when we learn the art of self-education we will find, if not create, opportunity to find success beyond our wildest dreams. Of course now a days technology available on the internet enables one to self-learn very fast without having the necessity to go to classes to study.

5. Harmonise natural talent with interest that motivates

Natural talent creates motivation, motivation creates persistence and persistence gets the job done. So, identifying one's own natural talents and nurturing them goes a long way in practicing motivation to do things well.

6. Increase knowledge of subjects that inspire

The more we know about a subject, the more we want to learn about it. We get in to a positive cycle of self upliftment that can take us to great heights of achievement and success in the long run.

7. Take risks

Failure and bouncing back are parts of normal living and indeed the key components of motivation. Failure is a learning tool. No one has ever succeeded at anything worthwhile without a string of failures. Great people like Abraham Lincoln or Scientists like Thomas Alva Edison are examples. Take calculated risks and keep learning from failures in order that the lessons can be moulded to pave the way for future success.

References

Books

A. 6. Keith Davis and J.W.Newstrom, "Human Behaviour at Work-Organizational Behaviour", Mcgraw-Hill, Newyirk, 1989.

A. 7. Fred Luthens, "Organisational Behaviour", Mcgraw Hill Inc., Newyork,1995.

A. 8. Dr. Anjali Ghanekar, "Organisational Behaviour, Concepts and Cases", Everest Publishing House, Pune, Eighth Edition, 2002.

Journals, Articles

B. 1. David C.Mclellend, "Managing Motivation to Expand Human Freedom", American Psychologist, 1978.

B. 2. Dr.Viswanathan Gopalan, "Motivation and Its Relevance to Productivity". Thesis for Ph.D, Pune University, 2001.

6

The Connection between Motivation and Performance in Work Places

'That some achieve great success, is proof to all that others can achieve it as well.'

Abraham Lincoln

'You must not lose faith in humanity. Humanity is an ocean; if a few drops of the ocean are dirty, the ocean does not become dirty.'

Mahatma Gandhi

Many business houses in India are re-organising themselves in order to cope with competition. Globalisation and growing internationalization, has tremendous impact on people management. The challenges include not only areas such as production or marketing or finance but also human resources functions such as recruitment, training etc.

In today's competitive environment, the organisations have to inculcate in to the people a desire to be innovative, creative and productive simultaneously. All this is possible only if people in any organisation remain motivated. The key to the entire issue of change has become the "motivation" of the people involved in the whole process of change and their willingness to be "productive" in an innovative way so as to beat the challenge the organisations face from competitors.

In this chapter, I have tried to share with the reader, the essence of my findings as a teacher and researcher, pertaining to the human factors or the motivational needs which contribute to enhanced performance, productivity and improved morale and happiness in work environments. The data and information obtained and analyzed have come from my original research on some of the industries, private and public both inclusive.

Productivity (Ref A. 5)

Definition of Productivity

1. Productivity is in-put and out-put ratio though in essence it is a process of harnessing the capacity to increase production by ensuring proper and efficient use of all types of resources to produce output at best quality, more volume and at lesser cost . The factors of production when combined with planned rationalistic organisation result into " productivity".
2. Productivity according to another expert is not merely volume of output nor a factor of production like land, labour, capital etc. nor even a technological or technical contrivance employed in industry. It is basically an instrument, which transforms a lagging world of production into a kicking entity. In a more summarized manner PRODUCTIVITY may be defined as Planned, Rationalistic, Organisation and Distribution of Constructive and Technical Ingredients-Variable for Intensive Technological Yoke.

Factors Affecting Productivity in a Work Place

Productivity is a multidimensional phenomenon. It depends on management, men, methods, machines and materials. As all the decisions about methods, machines and materials are made by management and executed by men, productivity very much depends upon management and men.

The management has to identify controllable and not so controllable factors of productivity. It is easy to identify controllable factors such as methods, machines, materials and money but it is difficult to apply the technique of productivity to man. The behaviour of man as an individual and as a member of a group is a fascinating subject to study. Men are governed by rational and not so rational thoughts, sentiments, emotions and motives. Men and their motivation are forever unpredictable and therefore difficult to control by a set of rules and regulations. This limitation has to be realistically accepted. Nevertheless a better understanding of men and their motivation will certainly help in increasing productivity. To say that productivity will increase by payment of higher wages or incentives or better supervision is to display a lack of appreciation to the multitude of motives and forces at work.

Productivity is adversely affected because of following:

- Failure to define objectives.
- Distrust
- Lack of delegation of power
- Improper work distribution
- Improper use of people and potentials

Relationship between Motivation and Productivity (Ref B. 2)

It is definitely established that improved motivation leads to improved performance and this in turn results in a reward situation for the employee both.

1. Extrinsic and
2. Intrinsic for the employee.

This in turn gives more job satisfaction the general consensus among researchers is that job satisfaction in the long run leads to improved productivity.

There are a few conditions under which high productivity is possible. One condition is that the employees perceive that the intrinsic and extrinsic rewards they obtain are as a result of their "productivity" and not based on other factors such as favoritism for a few. The second condition is that the extrinsic or external rewards must be distributed by the management to everyone in an equitable manner. In a situation where favoritism is felt and employees perceive that the external rewards like pay, promotion, special rewards etc., are given to individuals who are "loyal" to the top persons in a company and not to anyone who performs, employees may feel dissatisfied or even frustrated and that will be detrimental to collective performance and in turn results in decreased productivity in an organization.

This situation has, in fact, been explained well in the Porter-Lawler Model (Ref A.4) for motivation, performance and job satisfaction as illustrated in the following diagram.

Perceived Equity Rewards

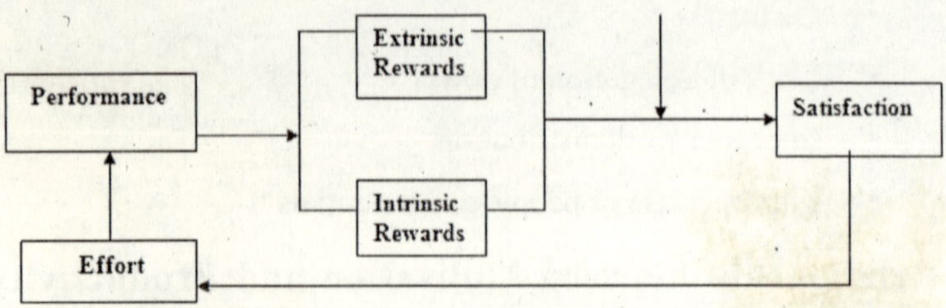

Fig. 5

Groups in Organizations and Productivity (Ref A. 4, B. 2)

According to theories on group formation in organisations, groups evolve in the following four stages which are:

1. Mutual acceptance
2. Communication and Decision Making
3. Motivation and Productivity and
4. Control and Organisation.

In the first two stages the members talk about themselves and their opinions accept each other and collectively begin to take decisions which ensure their survival in organisations. In the third, namely, the motivation and performing or productivity stage, the emphasis shifts from personal concerns or viewpoints to activities that will benefit the group. Members work together and accomplish common goals which not only help themselves but the organization as well. During this stage the members are highly motivated and may work together in creative ways. In the final stage, groups mature, group members are given tasks they are capable of achieving to their full potential and take corrective measures to reflect and improve performance of each and the group .

Group productivity depends on whether the groups evolve through all these stages effectively and whether they are matured. Members of productive groups will be independent, well organized and coordinated, efficient and highly motivated so that they produce at their best.

The aim of this book is to investigate issues pertaining to individual motivation, job satisfaction and group effectiveness on issues pertaining to productivity in organizations which include the private companies as well as public sectors.

Motivation and Performance (Ref B. 2)

In the foregoing chapters, the significance of the various types of motivational issues in human beings classified according to their needs as addressed in three contemporary theories on motivation namely,

1. Abraham Maslow's Need Hierarchy Theory

2. Herzberg's Two factor or Hygiene Theory of Motivation and

3. Mcclellend's 3N theory on Achievement, Affiliation and Power were introduced to the reader.

In this chapter, in the following paragraphs, in addition to what we explained as the connection between motivation and productivity through the Porter-Lawler Model, I have presented need wise, the answers to all the questions addressed in my investigation on human motivation and its effect on performance in work places.

The following is a summary of all those findings and my suggestions for improving human motivation and performance in work related situations.

Key Findings and Recommendations

1. The motivational theories of Abraham Maslow, McClelland and Herzberg are very much relevant to contemporary working in the industrial environment and human needs classified according to these theories do prevail in employees in various measures.
2. All the needs exist in all individuals in all age categories.
3. Each motivational need has relevance to productivity in individuals regardless of their age.
4. The most dominant motivational needs in individuals for the entire range of people investigated across different companies according to the percentage agreement figures compiled by the computer are given below in a descending order of dominance, even though they are concurrently present in individuals at the same time.

(a) Affiliation

(b) Recognition

(c) Esteem

(d) Belonging

(e) Achievement

(f) Physical/Security

(g) Actualisation

(h) Power

Affiliation and Recognition needs are the most important from the point of productivity and are at the top of the list while actualisation and power are the least dominant.

Esteem and belonging needs are very important for productivity and are more than achievement for productivity requirements. Physical and Security needs play a lot more role than actualization and power in motivating people to produce in work environments.

The following paragraphs list out the most important key findings and my recommendations grouped need wise for productivity improvements in Industries.

Affiliation as a Motivational Need for Productivity

The following table gives comparative data from private companies, public sectors and all companies on motivational issues pertaining to affiliation needs in so far as they affect productivity of employees.

S. No	Issue Under Scrutiny	Private Sector		Public Sector		All Companies		Remarks
		Yes Ans	Per-cent	Yes Ans	Per-cent	Yes Ans	Per-cent	
1.	Friendship of Peers Motivates individual to produce more	222	85.6	88	87.1	310	86.5	
2.	Participation in Image promotion of company improves productivity	215	83.6	81	80.1	296	82.6	
3.	Team work is a must for improving Productivity	195	75.8	85	84.1	280	78.2	
4.	Identifying with Company Needs enables people to produce more	197	76.6	78	77.2	275	76.8	
5.	Involvement of boss improves productivity	186	72.3	69	68.3	255	71.2	
6.	People do not like to work alone to produce	70	27.2	25	24.7	95	26.5	

Key Findings

The information presented in the above table clearly brings to our attention the following facts.

1. The employees of any organisation have a tremendous desire or need to get affiliated to the organization, in which they work, be it a private organisation or a public organisation.
2. Among the specific needs in question the uppermost or the most dominant appears to be need to be accepted by peers as part of the team and this seems to contribute to the

desire in the persons to produce better (85.1 Per cent private, 87.1 per cent public and 86.5 Per cent overall).

3. Getting involved at activities contributing to image building seems to fascinate most in both types of organisation (83.6 per cent private, 80.1 per cent public and 82.6 per cent overall). It is an eye opener to see that everybody is concerned about the image of the company they work in and would like to very much contribute to boosting it.
4. Team work is very critical to improved productivity (75.8 per cent in private, 84.1 per cent in public sectors, 78.2 per cent overall).
5. Involvement of the boss with subordinates is certainly a key factor contributing to productivity (72.3 percent private, 68.3 Percent public, 71.2 Percent overall) .
6. On the issue of working alone and producing only 26.5 percent overall have agreed that people do not like to work alone which implies that working alone or in team is not the issue people can still be productive. However, the earlier analysis indicates people prefer to work in teams. This opinion is the same in both private and public sectors as the percentages for agreement in opinion indicate.

Recommendations by the author for Productivity Improvement

- Employees must be made to feel wanted by involving them in decision making process.
- A participative type of environment must prevail in the organisation leading to improved productivity.
- Team work must be encouraged. Organisational missions and team goals must be clearly spelt to make people perform effectively.

Recognition as A Motivational Need for Productivity

The following table gives comparative data from private

companies, public sectors and all companies on motivational issues pertaining to recognition needs in so far as they affect productivity of employees.

S. No	Issue Under Scrutiny	Private Sector		Public Sector		All Companies		Remarks
		Yes's	Per-cent	yes's	Per-cent	Yes's	Per-cent	
1.	Promotion for excellent performance	218	84.8	91	90.1	309	86.5	
2.	Super performance rewards	219	85.2	88	87.1	307	85.9	
3.	Annual appraisal system to help improve performance	203	78.9	80	79.2	283	79.2	
4.	Yearly increments for performance	196	76.2	85	84.1	281	78.7	
5.	Rapid promotions for performance	187	72.7	75	74.2	262	73.3	
6.	Public recognition of employee	167	64.9	71	70.2	238	66.6	
7.	Punishments for non-performance	128	49.8	69	68.3	197	55.1	
8.	Money perks over non-financial perks for performance	130	50.5	44	43.5	174	48.7	
9.	Recognition by the immediate superior for performance	99	38.5	36	35.6	135	37.8	

Key Findings

The following are the facts which emerge by analyzing the above information:

1. Promotion for excellent performance stands out as the best motivator for productivity on an average in public and private

sectors. 86.5 per cent population of people surveyed has agreed to this point. However more percentage agreement has taken place in public sector units on this count than in private (90.1 per cent in public against 84.1 per cent in private).

2. Rewarding the employee for superior performance motivates them to produce more and this is equally so in public as well as private sector enterprises (85.2 per cent private and 87.1 per cent public sector). The overall percentage for all companies on this factor is 85.9 per cent.
3. Annual appraisal system for performance evaluation definitely help employees raise their performance levels for productivity according to almost an equal percentage of employees from public sector and private sector employees (78.9 per cent and 79.2 per cent) and all company average of 79.2 per cent.
4. Yearly increment for performance seems to motivate public sector employees a little more to perform than private sector employees (76.4 per cent – private, 84.1 per cent – public) . The overall percentage of people agreeing on this issue is 78.7 which is quite high indicating this to be a dominant recognition need deciding motivation of employees for productivity.
5. Rapid promotions for performance is a good motivator for performance according to an almost equal percentage of employees from private (72.7) and (74.2) per cent public sector employees.
6. Public recognition of an employee is a reasonably good motivator which enhances productivity in an organisation according to 64.2 per cent persons from private sector enterprises, 70.2 per cent from public sector and 66.6 per cent all companies put together.
7. Regarding punishment as a means to make people perform, less percentage of people tend to agree in private sectors

that this is effective (49.8) as against a fairly larger percentage in public sector (68.9) while the all company average remains at 55.1 per cent.

8. Money incentives as a means to perform over non-financial incentives does not seem to be so much of a favorite among people as indicated by a 50.5 per cent agreement from private sector employees, 43.5 from public sector individuals and 48.7 overall average. This can indicate that a mix of financial and non-financial perks in an equal fashion can motivate employees to produce more.
9. Recognition by the immediate superior for performance does not seem to a factor at all in motivating people to produce as only 38.5 per cent of private sector employees have agreed and 35.6 per cent from public sector have agreed. This may be compared with the need to be publicly recognized (All company average of 37.8 percent) . This indicates that the employees produce not for the boss but for the company or they would like to do so in order to be more productive.

Recommendations for Productivity Improvement

- Employees in an organisation must be quickly recognised for performance and be rewarded by special recognitions such as superior performance awards and promotions so that they can be motivated to become more productive.
- Annual appraisals and feedback will greatly enable the employee to improve himself and perform better.
- Yearly increments are good motivators even for normal performers to remain productive.
- Performing Employees must get public recognition.
- Punishments must not be used as means to make people produce. The author feels, on the contrary, it will generate an atmosphere of fear and hence people will shirk responsibilities and become less productive.

Esteem as A Motivational Need for Productivity

The following table gives comparative data from private companies, public sectors and all companies on motivational issues pertaining to esteem needs in so far as they affect productivity of employees.

S. No.	Issue Under Scrutiny	Private Sector		Public Sector		All Companies		Remarks
		Yes Ans	Per-cent	Yes Ans	Per-cent	Yes Ans	Per-cent	
1.	Job Enrichment improves esteem and productivity	234	91.0	94	93.0	328	91.6	
2.	Humiliating employees in front of others lowers esteem and productivity	217	84.4	81	80.1	298	83.2	
3.	Public recognition boosts esteem and production	194	75.4	80	79.2	273	76.2	
4.	Additional qualifications improve esteem, self-image and productivity	186	72.3	79	78.2	260	72.6	
5.	Rewards and Promotions improve esteem and productivity	180	70	67	66.3	253	70.6	
6.	Absence of interference from boss improves esteem and productivity	148	57.5	63	62.5	211	58.9	
7.	Status symbols improve esteem and productivity	137	53.3	51	50.4	188	52.5	
8.	Constant attention by the boss boosts esteem and hence productivity	94	36.5	44	43.5	138	38.5	
9.	Being told to do often by the boss boosts improves self-esteem and productivity	77	29.9	39	38.6	116	32.4	

Key Findings

The following inferences are possible from the above data presented.

1. Job enhancement improves self-esteem and productivity considerably according to the opinion of a very high percentage of employees both in private and public enterprises (91 per cent private, 93 per cent public and 91.6 per cent all companies average).

2. Employees do not like to be humiliated in front of others. This lowers their esteem and contributes to loss of production and hence productivity (84.4, 80.1 and 83.2 per cent in private, public and all respectively).
3. Publicly recognising the employee certainly boosts the esteem and hence the productivity levels of the employee (75.4 percent private, 79.2 per cent public, 76.2 per cent all) Opinion is sort of uniform this being a little stronger with regard to public sector employees.
4. Additional qualification certainly contribute to building self image and esteem of the employee in both kinds of organizations (72.3 per cent private, 78.6 percent public, per cent 78.6 all).
5. Rewards and promotions certainly contribute to improved esteem and productivity as 70 per cent from private and 66.3 from public have agreed, 70.6 per cent being the overall average.
6. A fairly large percentage, though not very high (58.9 per cent from all companies) think that the boss should not interfere in the subordinate's work and that improves the self-esteem of the individual which leads to improved productivity.
7. Status symbols like a cabin or car do not contribute very much to productivity or the opinion is divided on this issue as only 53.3 per cent from private units, 50.4 per cent from public sector companies and 52.5 per cent (all company average) from all companies say so. This seems to be a uniform opinion right across all companies.
8. Constant attention by the boss is absolutely not contributive to productivity as the opinion from private companies (36.5 per cent) public units (43.5 per cent) indicate.
9. Being given instructions constantly also does not boost either the esteem or productivity levels in companies as the opinions from all companies clearly demonstrate (29.9 per cent from

private, 38.6 per cent from public sector, 32.4 per cent from all companies).

Recommendations for Productivity Improvement (Ref B. 2)

- Self-esteem of an employee is very important and significant from the point of view of improving his productivity and hence that of the organization.
- The management must from time to time review the contents of the job of each employee and try and enrich it so that the employee feels satisfied and motivated to work more.
- Public recognition of an employee is a great esteem and productivity.
- A fair and just reward and promotion system must be in place in an organisation. A timely reward or promotion is more than enough to make an employee feel happy so that he gives out his best.
- An employee must never ever be humiliated in front of others, the research reveals clearly as it kills his esteem completely.
- Superiors must delegate and trust in their assistants and not constantly interfere or give instructions. Freedom to perform and encouragement will go a long way in improving productivity.

Belonging as A Motivational Need for Productivity

The following table gives comparative data from private companies, public sectors and all companies on motivational issues pertaining to belonging needs in so far as they affect productivity of employees.

S. No	Issue Under Scrutiny	Private Sector		Public Sector		All Companies		Remarks
		Yes Ans	Per-cent	Yes Ans	Per-cent	Yes Ans	Per-cent	
1.	Team goal for motivation and productivity	239	92.9	91	90.1	330	92.1	
2.	Better communication between boss and sub-ordinate	205	79.7	73	72.2	278	77.6	
3.	Being part of a team improves productivity	146	56.8	71	70.2	217	60.6	
4.	Sharing of personal problems with people improves productivity	125	48.6	60	59.4	185	51.6	
5.	Emotional closeness with the boss for performance	123	47.8	51	50.4	174	48.6	
6.	Visiting each other after office hours improves relationship for performance	123	47.8	49	48.5	172	48.0	
7.	Conducting parties in the office frequently improves relationship and hence productivity	112	43.5	24	23.7	136	37.9	

Key Findings

The following key inferences are possible from the data presented above:

1. People are motivated not only when they work in teams but when they know the direction in which they are going (Team Goal). This opinion is equally prevalent both in public sectors and in private sectors as indicated by the percentage opinions gathered through the questionnaire (92.9 private, 90.1 public and 90.2 all companies).

2. Better communication between superiors and sub-ordinates is essential for improved performance and productivity. The

private sector employees express this opinion a little more strongly than the public sector employees (79.7 private, 72.2 public and 77.6 percent all companies).

3. Being a member of a team merely instead of being alone improves productivity according to 56.6 per cent from private sector, 70.2 per cent from public sectors and 60.6 per cent an overall percentage.
4. Sharing personal problems with people is neither a great booster for productivity nor a factor to be ignored. It is to be noted that only 48.6 per cent from private sector, 59. 4 from public sector and 51.6 per cent from all units have agreed that sharing personal problems with others improves productivity.
5. Emotional closeness with the boss – Does it contribute to productivity or does it enhance performance? The opinion is uniform across companies as the percentages for agreement indicate, viz., 47.8 from private sector, 50.4 from public units and all company average of 48.6. Obviously this factor is not a great performance enhancer.
6. Visiting each other after office hours does not so much motivate people for improved production as only 47.8 percent from private units, 48.5 from public sector and 48.0 percent from across all companies have agreed to this view. The opinion is uniform across all companies.
7. Conducting parties in a work environment, which we observe in several companies, which the managements believe improves camaraderie and hence will result in improved production does not seem to be so. Only 43.5 percent from private sector, a meager 23.7 per cent from public sector and 37.1 per cent across all companies agree that this is a motivator for productivity at all . It is very surprising, even to the author, why so many companies are encouraging this practice. The survey indicates that it is a myth that parties in a work place do not motivate people to be more efficient.

Recommendations for Productivity Improvement

- Improving communication among people in general and especially between bosses and sub-ordinates, making team goals clear to members of teams helps improve productivity in a work environment greatly.
- People may be allowed to share personal problems with others to a certain extent without making them feel very much concerned about "professionalism" in a work place. This can lead to a certain "unburdening" of emotions and can contribute to improved performance. However, this may not be a major contributor to productivity.
- The time, money and efforts spent by companies to organize parties to bring people together may be reduced both inside and outside works. People should be made to help and work together to feel closer and produce more.

Achievement as A Motivational Need for Productivity

The following table gives comparative data from private companies, public sectors and all companies on motivational issues pertaining to achievement needs in so far as they affect productivity of employees.

No	Issue Under Scrutiny	Private Sector		Public Sector		All Companies		Remarks
		Yes Ans	Percent	Yes Ans	Percent	Yes Ans	Percent	
1	Greater sense of achievement through production	235	91.4	90	89.1	325	90.7	
2	Clear career goals improve productivity	200	77.8	74	73.2	274	76.5	
3	Big assignments with rewards enhance performance	179	69.6	57	56.4	236	65.9	
4	Rapid promotions with money	136	52.9	51	50.4	187	52.2	
5	Status symbols enhance a sense of achievement and hence productivity	129	50.1	33	32.6	162	45.2	
6	Reaching the top at the earliest is an achievement goal improving productivity	105	40.8	34	33.6	139	38.8	
7	People feel frustrated when they do not get promoted and stop producing	29	11.2	11	10.8	40	11.1	

Key Findings

The following key inferences are possible from the data presented above:

1. People in all companies, be it a private sector company or a public sector unit are keen to produce more, because that itself gives them a sense of pride and achievement as 91.4 per cent in private companies, 89.1 in public companies and 90.7 in all companies put together have said in the affirmative. This implies that people must be given a lot of productive work and they will happily work.
2. Clear career goals excite people to produce well and in this also the opinions are fairly uniform across private and public

companies (77.8 Per cent private, 73.2 Per cent public and 76.5 Per cent all companies).

3. Big assignments assuring people clear rewards are fairly good motivators for productivity as the research reveals as do the table. 69.6 per cent from private companies, 56.4 percent from public sector units and 65.5 per cent from across all companies have subscribed to this view. It is to be noted that the public sector employees have expressed a slightly smaller percentage opinion in this regard than the private sector guys. This can be interpreted as the presence of less opportunities of this kind in those units than in private units and hence people there have accepted not to expect the same in any big way compared to their counterparts in private sector companies.
4. Rapid promotions with increased money rewards may not be a high motivator for enhancing productivity, but, none the less it is a good enough factor to motivate people to produce more as 52.9 per cent people from private sectors, 50.4 from public and 52.2 per cent from across all companies have agreed.
5. Not many people seem to agree that status symbols such as a car or cabin enhances the sense of achievement which in turn can motivate the person to produce more. 50.1 percent from private companies, 32.6 only from public sectors and 45.2 per cent across all companies have subscribed to this view.
6. Reaching the top early in life is not regarded as a great achievement nor does it motivate people to produce more. Only 40.6 per cent from private enterprises and 33.6 from public sectors feel that it is an achievement to reach the top early and it does motivate someone to be more productive. The all company average on this opinion in 38.8 per cent. It is a wonder why companies are trying to push so many young people to the top now days instead of working on issues like job enrichment etc.

7. Promotion as an issue is not a great motivator which propels people to produce more. Only 11.2 per cent from private sector and 10.8 per cent from public sector have agreed that they feel frustrated if they do not get promotions and stop producing as a result. The all company average is 11.1 percent on this opinion.

Recommendations for Productivity Improvement (Ref B. 2)

- All must be given meaningful jobs to work and that itself will be regarded as achievement by them because they really want to work.
- People want to aim for clear career goals and management must help their employees to set these goals and achieve them.
- People must be given big assignment with assurances of clear rewards and must not be tested on insignificant work with no rewards. Good assignments and good perceivable rewards motivate people to produce more.
- People on the fast track may not be "Role Models" inciting others to produce because people do not seem to regard rapid promotions as big achievements. Perhaps, the "loop holes" in the promotion systems in corporate work places in India are well known to all employees in all enterprises.
- Excess expenditure in providing status symbols such as car or cabin or secretaries must be eliminated because these are not contributing to improvement in performance.

Physical/Security Needs as Motivational Needs for Productivity

The following table gives comparative data from private companies, public sectors and all companies on motivational issues pertaining to security needs in so far as they affect productivity of employees.

S. No	Issue Under Scrutiny	Private Sector		Public Sector		All Companies		Remarks
		Yes Ans	Per-cent	Yes Ans	Per-cent	Yes Ans	Per-cent	
1.	Good transportation improves motivation and productivity	227	88.3	84	83.1	311	86.8	
2.	Good canteen facilities	213	82.8	82	81.1	295	82.4	
3.	Good health care facilities	182	70.8	87	86.1	269	75.1	
4.	A good salary hike motivates people to work more	170	66.1	70	69.3	240	67.0	
5.	Long term benefits like super annuation improve motivation to produce	145	56.4	79	78.2	224	62.5	
6.	Life time security in a job prompts people to produce more	161	62.6	63	62.3	224	62.5	
7.	Educational allowance contributes to improved motivation and hence productivity	160	62.2	58	57.4	218	60.8	
8.	Housing amenities for all employees improves morale and performance	138	53.6	70	69.3	208	58.1	
9.	The role of uniforms in motivation	129	50.1	60	59.4	189	52.7	
10.	Time scale promotions reduce favoritism, leads to job satisfaction and improves productivity	91	35.4	48	47.5	139	38.8	

Key Findings

The following are the key findings with respect to the information tabulated above.

1. The first and primary observation by the Author is that Herzberg's two factor theory seems to be in question wherein he says environmental factors are not necessarily motivators but can be "de-motivators" if they are not provided. The people surveyed in this research clearly have given a verdict that many of these factors are positive "motivators" which are analyzed for their effect on productivity.
2. A good transportation facility for carrying employees from houses to works and back is a great motivator which reminds people to stay productive. This fact has been acknowledged by 88.3 per cent from private sector, 83.1 from public sector and 86.8 per cent from all companies.
3. Good Canteen facilities are a must for people to eat well which in turn leads to a sense of satisfaction which contributes to the opinion the employees hold about the company and the management which turn makes people a lot more productivity. It is very surprising and rather startling to know that 82.8 per cent people from private sectors, 81.1 per cent from public sectors and 82.4 per cent from all companies surveyed have subscribed to this view. Many companies run canteen services but are not focusing on the facilities inside or the quality of food not knowing that this is a great motivator which impels people to produce. The need we are addressing here is hunger which is a basic instinct well addressed by Maslow need is his hierarchy theory as a "drive" which motivates people while the two factor theory of Herzberg gives it only an environmental status since canteen is environmental. The author is convinced that these needs are very much motivators and are key factors contributing to productivity in a work environment.
4. Good health care facilities to employees are a must for motivation and productivity improvement (70.8 per cent - private, 86.1 percent - public and 75.1 per cent -all companies).

5. Life time security in a job is a reasonable factor which motivates people to stay on and produce more as indicated by the table 62.6 per cent from private companies, 62.3 per cent from public sectors and 62.5 per cent from all companies. We can regard this as a reasonably powerful tool to motivate people to produce in today's scenario where people change jobs often .
6. Perks like educational allowance (60.8 per cent –all company figure for agreement) and housing amenities (58.1 per cent agreement from all companies) do also seem to be good motivators as the percentage of people from all industries indicates.
7. Making every one wear the same uniform does not have a profound impact on productivity as indicated by the opinions from private sector persons (50.1 per cent), public sector employees (59.4 per cent) and all companies (52.7 percent). However, this factor cannot be ruled out as minor so far as motivation is concerned. The author's own experience is that uniforms do make people belong to one large family and hence the level differences perceived in organisations are minimised when everybody wears the same uniform and hence people co-operate with each other more to produce.
8. People do not believe time scale promotions reduce favouritism and hence motivate people to be more productive. Only 35.4 per cent from private sector, 47.5 per cent from public companies and 38.8 per cent from all companies have agreed to the view that time scale promotions reduce favouritism and leads to motivation and productivity.

Recommendations of The Author for Productivity Improvement (Ref B. 2)

- The companies must provide good transportation, good canteen facilities and good health care schemes in order to motivate people stay physically or psychologically secured which will in turn lead to improved productivity in the work environment.

- Lifetime security measures like PF or Super Annuation do provide motivation for employees to stay productive. These facilities may be made a little more attractive as the employee towards the end of his career looks forward to a peaceful retired life. These facilities may prompt a younger employee definitely think twice before he opt out of a company to move in to another.

Actualisation as A Motivational Need for Productivity

S. No	*Issue Under Scrutiny*	*Private Sector*		*Public Sector*		*All Companies*		*Remarks*
		Yes Ans	*Percent*	*Yes Ans*	*Percent*	*Yes Ans*	*Percent*	
1.	Common goals of the company motivates people to produce more	187	72.7	84	83.1	271	75.6	
2.	Job Satisfaction motivates people to produce more	167	64.9	77	76.2	244	68.1	
3.	Discovery of self through the job motivates for production	156	60.7	85	84.1	241	67.3	
4.	People work for the sheer love of their job	153	59.5	69	68.3	222	62	
5.	The overall happiness of people Motivates one to work	144	56	73	72.2	217	60.6	
6.	Contributing to society makes people produce	138	53.6	58	57.2	196	54.7	
7.	Work for the sake of work (Karma)	135	52.5	56	55.4	191	53.3	
8.	Excelling in job motivates people to produce	134	52.1	51	50.4	185	51.6	
9.	People will sacrifice anything in personal life for the job	45	17.5	27	26.7	72	20.1	

This need is almost at the bottom of the list of dominant needs just a little above power as graph indicates. The following table gives consolidated information regarding the relevance of actualisation needs of employees from various companies with regard to their productivity.

Key Findings

The following are the key findings with regard to actualisation needs in people which can be motivators to productivity.

1. Identification with the common goals of the company is the highest motivator in this category of needs with 72.7 per cent from private, 83.1 per cent from public and 75.6 per cent from all companies agreeing to this view. This question has been dealt with in other categories of needs such as affiliation etc. However, here, it is treated as an actualisation need presuming that the individual regards the company as a life giver of all sorts.
2. If people are satisfied with the job they hold and do, they produce more. This is the opinion given by 64.9 per cent people from private organisations, 76.2 per cent from public organisations and 68.1 per cent from all companies.
3. Discovery of the self, the highest level need in individuals, at least according to the ancient Indian philosophies, is something quite a few seem to practice in order to be productive and useful. That is a view expressed by 60.7 per cent from private companies, 84.1 per cent from public companies and 67.3 per cent from all companies.
4. Do people work for the sheer love of their job? 59.5 per cent from private sectors have said so. This view is endorsed by 68.2 per cent from public sectors. The all company agreement on this count is 62 per cent.
5. Contributing to the happiness of everyone seems to be an actualisation need which a fair amount of people cherish as indicated by the full agreement percentage figures of 56, 72.2 and 60.6 for private, public and all companies respectively.

6. Contributing to society at large is an average motivator for productivity. This is evident from the figures 53.6 percent from private sector employees, 57.2 from public sectors and an all company percentage of 54.7. People seem to be thinking about people, not about society in a big way.
7. Are people working because work is worship or because work is " karma" or "work for the sake of work"? An average level of agreement is indicated by the figures 52.5 percent from private sectors, 55.4 from public and 53.3 per cent from across all companies. Quite a lot of companies try and glorify and brain wash people in to believing work – any work is worship. Sadly, not everyone seems to be falling for this idea, though quite a few seem to agree.
8. Working towards excellence seems to be an average motivator for improving productivity. This is confirmed by the percentage agreement figures of 52.1, 50.4 and 52.6 for private, public and all companies respectively. Again, the author would like to note that companies talk quite a lot about driving people towards the mythical "excellence" while the normal man is not so much impressed by those catch words. He is down to earth and very practical as this research clearly reveals.
9. Nobody really wants to sacrifice anything in personal life for the sake of the job and sacrificing personal things does not contribute to productivity. Only 17.5 per cent from private sectors, 26.7 per cent from public companies and 20.1 from all companies have agreed that they think sacrificing personal things in life contributes to improving productivity in work places. Will the Indian companies learn from this finding which is quite startling? Every owner believes he owns the employee because he pays and so 24 hours a day he is expected to be at the beck and call of the employer. It

contributes to production in no way and not many agree that it does.

Recommendations for Productivity Improvement (Ref B. 2)

- Companies must often communicate to the employees regarding their immediate and long term goals and missions so that all employees can identify with them and feel actualised to join the drive to realize those dreams. This will go a long way in improving productivity levels in a company.
- People must be given jobs and responsibilities in which they can realise themselves and feel happy and satisfied. Slotting people to jobs which they do not want to do may be the easiest way to bring morale and productivity levels down. Making people do jobs they like best is the best way to boost productivity levels in a company.
- Big jargon like "Excellence" or work for "everybody else" do not motivate people to produce so much more. The author strongly recommends that the companies must stop talking too much about excellence. The people know how they should excel and to what extent. The need should come from within and the companies should facilitate the process and not compel them.
- People should be encouraged to keep their personal lives in tact and not sacrifice for the company. The author feels this amounts to exploitation. The research reveals nobody wants to sacrifice personal lives to go up in career. If at all a few are doing it, it can be out a fear of failure or compulsions of not losing a job. People do not perform in jobs just by sacrificing anything precious to their personal lives. On the contrary, the author strongly feels, if the companies care about the personal lives of their employees, the employees will voluntarily cooperate to produce efficiently and assist in times of crises.

Power as A Motivational Need for Productivity

The following table gives comparative data from private companies, public sectors and all companies on motivational issues pertaining to power needs in so far as they affect productivity of employees.

S. No	Issue Under Scrutiny	Private Sector		Public Sector		All Companies		Remarks
		Yes Ans	Per-cent	Yes Ans	Per-cent	Yes Ans	Per-cent	
1.	More responsibilities with more authority make people produce more	196	76.2	82	81.1	278	77.6	
2.	Reaching a position Helps people to contribute to productivity	196	76.2	78	77.2	274	76.5	
3.	Quick promotions and more powers for better performance	121	47	41	40.5	162	45.2	
4.	More people below and more power helps one to perform better	119	46.3	35	34.6	154	43.0	
5.	Support of strong peer group helps productivity	90	35	44	43.5	134	37.4	
6.	Empowerment helps people to produce more	58	22.5	20	19.8	78	21.7	
7.	The role of a God Father in Productivity	43	16.7	19	18.8	62	17.3	

Key Findings

The following are the key findings with regard to factors deciding power motivation needs in so far as they affect productivity in individuals in private, public and all types of companies.

1. Giving more responsibilities coupled with authority make people produce more. This opinion is uniform right across all companies, be it private or public. The opinion poll indicates the following percentages namely 76.2 per cent for private, 81.1 per cent for public companies and 77.6 per cent for all companies.
2. People want to reach positions of authority in order that they can contribute to productivity more. This opinion is endorsed by 76.2 per cent from private sector personnel, 77.2 per cent from public sector employees and 76.5 per cent from the total employees surveyed from all companies. The opinion is uniform across all companies.
3. Quick promotions help acquire more power in order to perform is a view accepted by not many. 47 per cent from private companies and 40.5 per cent from public sectors have agreed that this is true.
4. Keeping many people below increases the power base and helps do more work is a view not accepted by many in both private and public sectors as the percentage agreement table of 46.3 for private companies and 34.6 for public companies indicate. The all company table for this opinion is a mere 43 percent.
5. Support of peer groups in order to muster power does not seem to motivate people to produce more. 35 per cent from private sectors and 43.5 per cent from public sectors have agreed that the support of a strong peer group contributes in any way to productivity.
6. Now we come to an interesting need, namely the need to be empowered. It is surprising that only 22.5 of those surveyed from private sector companies, 19.8 from public sectors and 21.7 per cent from across all companies have agreed that this is a motivational need which if fulfilled can lead to improved productivity. This leads us to believe that in a work environment it is not enough if people are "delegated powers to perform" but the right psychological

environment which will foster a sense of affiliation, give recognition to individuals, boost their ego and self-esteem needs will contribute a lot more to productivity.

7. It looks as if " God fathers" of individuals do not play any role in motivating people to produce more. Only 16.7 per cent of the surveyees from private sectors, 18.8 per cent from public sectors and 17.3 per cent of people from across all companies have agreed that God fathers do play a role in individual's productivity in work places. Then the question arises as to why there is so much emphasis on authority and control in corporate work environment? The author's opinion is that hierarchy contributes very little to improving productivity. A horizontal, matrix kind of an organisation will be a lot more productive than a vertical organisation where there are more chances of " God fatherism " prevailing at every level.

Recommendations for Productivity Improvement (Ref B. 2)

- All employees in an organisation must be given not only responsibilities but also authority to carry out tasks. This should not be achieved by quickly promoting a few to positions of authority. At each level enough responsibility combined with authority makes a job lot more challenging.The environment can become a lot more productive this way.
- Mustering muscle power does not contribute to productivity. It may be recalled that under affiliation needs peer support is a strong factor for productivity enhancement. However, when it comes to "Power Politics", it is detrimental to productivity.
- Vertical, hierarchy based, bureaucratic organisations are non-productive and they also encourage "God fathers" to protect their wards who may be unproductive. A matrix type of organisation devoid of "God Fathers" is an ideal

place for production and improved productivity.

Motivation and productivity are factors closely linked in the human environment in work places It has been evident that the contemporary, content theories on motivation such as (1) Maslow's Need Hierarchy Model (2) Herzberg's two factor theory on motivation and (3) McClelland's 3n theory about Achievement, Affiliation and Power, are very much applicable to the motivational issues in industries of the present day and that they very much affect productivity in any age group .

The interesting finding is that achievement and power needs are important but not so much as other needs such as affiliation, Recognition, Esteem and belonging to propel people for greater productivity. In fact, the one thing that stands out from the investigation is that affiliation and recognition needs of employees are the most important and top the list of needs for productivity issues across all age groups on all industries and they must be addressed by managements if they have to make people produce more.

The following graph illustrates the overall impact of human needs in making them become more productive to perform in work environments in general.

Recommendations for general motivation and productivity improvements have been given by the author, which are applicable to any industry. The author wishes to pass on the knowledge obtained through the investigation, to the Human Resources Departments of organisations and the leaders in them so that it becomes fruitful in paving the way for greater motivation, performance improvement and creation of on a happy, innovative environment.

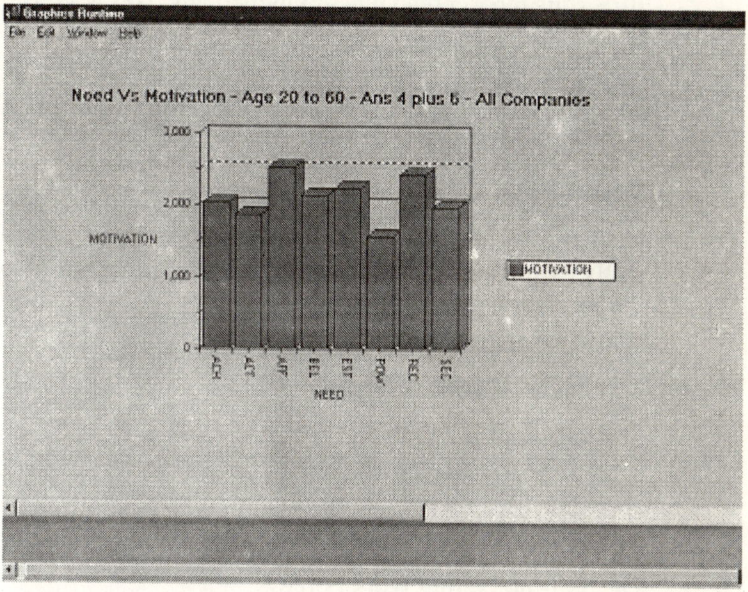

Fig. 6

The author wishes to share with the reader some of the key leadership issues involved in generating a motivating, self-empowering work environment which contributes to greater performance and the collective well being of the human beings involved in the entire process.

Motivation, Empowerment and Leadership

The modern leader does not believe in the command and control type of leadership, but is a firm believer in motivating and empowering people to perform. This he achieves by setting a self-example for others to follow. "He believes in having "Willing Followers". He is also a visionary and a story teller. The following are some of the key issues in motivating and empowering employees in work places for better performance.

- A Distinctive company image - strong company personalities attract and repel certain types of individuals. This is a result of company's policies, practices, or priorities. Company personality is built and maintained by combining motivation, opportunity, and creating a desire to learn. The result, a super motivated environment.

- Motivation Management

  Leaders must have teaching and coaching skills, not control skills. Motivated people have goals and seek ways to achieve them. Efficiency and effectiveness is the result of motivated employees.

- Continuous Learning Opportunity

  Motivation is associated with the desire to learn. There needs to be growth opportunity. Without it motivation dies. Providing a learning environment is the responsibility of the leader.

- The Self-motivating Work Force

  Employees must be trained to assume responsibility for their tasks and must be given sufficient authority to carry out those tasks. An environment where employees trust management and management trust workers should be the ideal vision of a leader.

- The Self-Educating Work Force

  With fast changing technology, the only way to acquire new skills that stays ahead of the competition is through self-education and team-education. Knowledge must be acquired as it comes into the marketplace from its source. Educational institutions offer advance technology courses only when there is a demand for it. By that time, much of its competitive value is gone. The organizations should collaborate with educational institutions to change this scenario.

- Knowledge Worker

Most businesses operate with a wide knowledge gap between worker and management. All through history this has been the policy and that it is job security for leadership. Today, efficiency requires knowledge workers to assume responsibility. This is achieved by empowering knowledge workers, recognising and rewarding them to stay motivated and productive.

References books

A.5. Shyam Gokhale," Personnel Management and Organizational Behaviour", Publisher, Mrs. Susheel Gokhale, 1st Edition, 1961

A.6.Keith Davis and J.W.Newstrom," Human Behaviour at Work-Organisational Behaviour", Mcgraw - Hill, Newyirk,1989

A.8. Dr.Anjali Ghanekar," Organizational behaviour, Concepts and Cases", Everest Publishing House, Pune, Eighth Edition, 2002

Journals, Articles

B.1. David C. Mclellend,' Managing Motivation to expand Human Freedom",American Psychologist, 1978

B.2. Dr.Viswanathan Gopalan," Motivation and Its Relevance to Productivity".Thesis for Ph.D, Pune University, 2001.

7

Knowledge Management and Motivation- the Connection

'Innovation comes only from readily and seamlessly sharing information rather than hoarding it.'

-Tom Peters

'Wise men appreciate all men, for they see the good in each and how hard it is to make anything good'

- Baltasar Gracian

Knowledge and Knowledge Management

Information represents the idea of translating pieces of data we encounter regularly in our lives with relationships among them so that we can make meaningful interpretations of those isolated pieces of data in to understandable forms which we designate as 'Information' for our convenience.

Knowledge on the other hand crosses boundaries of information and delves in to 'understanding' 'patterns' across large chunks of information around us, some of which may be irrelevant sometimes. In order that we can derive conclusions as to how things are happening the way they occur.

Information refers to description, definition or perspectives of objects and events we encounter-like what, who, when and where while knowledge comprises of strategies, approaches and methods – as to how things occur.

When we go deep in to issues like why things occur the way they do and why not differently, we graduate from knowledge and begin to merge in to the world of 'Wisdom'.

In fact, the transition from data to information to knowledge and then wisdom is one continuum without clear boundaries and the borders merge and blur as we move from one process in to another.

This paper tries to discuss in detail the challenge of 'Managing Knowledge' for beneficial and useful purposes in a work environment by encouraging the so called 'Knowledge Worker' to stay 'Motivated' and productive so that he and the organisation will benefit fulfilling the organisational vision, mission and objective and goals in the long run.

A very elaborate discussion of both topics namely 'Knowledge Management' and 'Motivation' in work spaces follows while the author attempts to integrate the concepts which will achieve the purpose the title of this chapter envisages, namely 'Motivating the Knowledge Worker' in Organisations and work places.

The points discussed in this chapter are applicable to all the corporates, private and public, academic institutions, medium sised companies in the private sector and NGOs.

Definition of Knowledge Management

1. 'Knowledge management refers to strategies and structures for maximizing the return on intellectual and information resources. Because intellectual capital resides both in tacit form (human education, experience and expertise) and explicit form (documents and data), KM depends on both cultural and technological processes of creation, collection, sharing, recombination and reuse of knowledge. The goal is to create a new value by improving the efficiency and effectiveness of individual and collaborative knowledge work while increasing innovation and sharpening decision making.'

2. 'Knowledge management is the practice of harnessing and exploiting intellectual capital to gain competitive advantage and customer commitment through efficiency, innovation, faster and more effective decision-making.'

KM is a new, recent way of looking at the way any business or an organisation needs to define its own mission or vision in an indirect manner.

Knowledge Management in Business

KM implies managing KNOWLEDGE ASSETS well in order to achieve the visions/missions/goals of an organisation.

Knowledge Assets of an Organisation

(a) All processes, all applications, all projects

(b) All Customers

(c) All Vendors

(e) All Employees

(f) All 'Knowledge Workers'

We will be focusing on the role of the knowledge worker in the process of an organisation managing its knowledge to fulfill its goals and missions and the need to keep him motivated so that he does not leave the organisation which could imply a loss not only in terms of innovativeness and knowledge but really in terms of productivity and profitability in the long run.

The Two Types of Knowledge Sources

1. **Explicit** : This knowledge is available in written format in documental forms like books or articles or stored in a medium like a computer or its memory devices of various categories.
2. **Tacit** : It is in the minds of the human beings in an organization. These knowledge assets not written or stored.

Managing explicit knowledge can be done with technology. Managing Tacit knowledge is difficult since it is left entirely with the individual to Share. This is where a knowledge worker comes in to picture.

Knowledge Worker

A knowledge worker is a person identified in an organisation in a specific practice area or a functional area or a domain who is qualified adequately, skilled or experienced to do the activities meant to be carried in his area of expertise and also capable of Sharing and Training other people to distribute and re-use the knowledge among every one including new comers so that the entire team gets the benefit of the knowledge to fulfil team goals and objectives. It could be the carrying out of a simple project to achieving the annual targets in a specific domain for a specific activity.

Nowadays, an organisation implements a structure for knowledge management in which the content managers and technical teams are separately identified and structured departmental wise to carry out both tasks. The content developer teams are classified area wise and designations such as 'Knowledge workers', 'Knowledge champions' or 'Knowledge gurus' are assigned to individuals depending upon the roles they play and the levels of commitment and skills they exhibit

The role of a knowledge worker

There are a few important roles a knowledge worker can play effectively on an organisation. They are:

1. Sharing his/her existing knowledge with others for re-use.
2. Bring in new knowledge for innovation and improved efficiency and productivity.
3. Train other potential knowledge people to become future knowledge workers.
4. Improve the 'Motivation' and 'Morale' of the environment for greater levels of performance.
5. Act as role model leaders of the organization propelling it towards greater participation in contributing to social causes and society at large improving awareness of people and the management in aspects such as 'Corporate social Responsibility' and 'Accountability' to the public and the world at large.

Motivating the Knowledge Worker –Importance

When organisations decide to implement 'Knowledge Management' as a policy or a strategy for survival and progress, there are some challenges they need to address while doing so. They are, as we discussed a little earlier,

1. Identifying 'Knowledge Workers'
2. Empowering them to contribute to the knowledge environment.
3. Creating a technical infrastructure with IT Tools like, servers, portals where people can log in, access and input sharable knowledge
4. Building teams for knowledge sharing through common platforms.
5. Organising seminars and conference for knowledge sharing.

The most challenging of all the measures mentioned above is the task of recognising, rewarding and motivating the Key Knowledge Workers so that they themselves do not think of leaving the organization and going elsewhere where their skills, talents and knowledge can be more beneficially and productively utilized and they in turn get appropriately rewarded, both intrinsically and extrinsically to their own satisfaction. Motivating the knowledge worker is important in a work place because it results in the following advantages.

1. Improved Innovation.
2. Less Attrition.
3. Improved motivation and Morale for all people.
4. Increased Productivity.
5. An enhanced brand equity.
6. Profitability and sustainability in the long run.

The Main Challenges in Motivating the Knowledge Worker

From the previous chapter which discussed in detail, some of the key findings on motivating people in work environments for productivity, through the research done by the author, the following inferences can be drawn regarding motivating the knowledge worker in an organisation.

1. Identifying and recognising the knowledge worker in itself of primary importance. A systematic collection of the data regarding the qualifications and skills of the knowledgeable people is done and a 'Data Base' has to be built to identify the best.
2. Involve or 'Affiliate' those people in activities related to collection and storage of knowledge in the 'Knowledge Management' tools or 'platforms' or 'servers' for ready access by all people. Information technology enables building these 'Portals' which can be used for storage and retrieval of vital 'documents' which are 'explicit' in nature.
3. Appoint a top level champion among the Knowledge workers, assign the full responsibility of coordinating the knowledge management activities of the place and give him sufficient powers and support to carry out the Knowledge Management activities..
4. Build teams of knowledge workers in different functional domains and encourage them to 'share'.
5. Conduct periodical meets, conferences, workshops and talks by experts both from inside and outside the organisation for knowledge sharing and dissemination among employees.
6. Incentives for knowledge sharing are very important.

Example of a Corporate in India which has successfully Implemented KM

This is an IT company in India which is well known for its contribution to the economy. It has a good knowledge management structure. The company has an environment for motivating knowledge workers and provides incentives to motivate and retain them in order to sustain innovativeness and productivity in the company. A few strategies the company adopts for this purpose, very briefly are:

- Allowing employees to participate in the acquisition, submission, reviewing and re-use of knowledge assets.
- Incentives for this kind of 'knowledge sharing'.
- Periodic K-Summits for celebrating knowledge sharing activities and to publicly recognise and reward the leaders in knowledge sharing.

Summary and Conclusion

Motivating the knowledge worker involves the task of creating a technical and administrative infrastructure for the purpose. The job involves identifying knowledge workers and champions in several functional areas of the organisation and empowering them to perform by affiliating them in decision making, recognising and rewarding them so that they can contribute to building a grand 'knowledge repository' which is a wealth of knowledge derived from the past, re-usable in the present and will lead to innovation, improved performance, greater productivity, reduction in attrition and finally enhanced brand equity and profitability. The greatest challenge in front of any management is to make people 'share knowledge'. If that is achieved, the rest of the benefits follow. It becomes a win-win situation for all the stake holders.

References

Journals

B.1. David C. "Mclellend,' Managing Motivation to expand Human Freedom", American Psychologist, 1978

B.2. Dr. Viswanathan Gopalan, "Motivation and Its Relevance to Productivity". Thesis for Ph.D, Pune University, 2001

B.3. Fred Luthens and Robert Krietner, "The Management of Behavioural Contingencies", Personnel, July 1974

B.4. Frederick Hertzberg, One More Time, "How do you

Motivate Employees", Harvard Business Review, Selected Articles, Reprint, Motivation,1970

B.5. Dr Viswanathan Gopalan, "Motivating Knowledeg Worker". ISSN-Journal Symbiosis, 2012

8
Stress Management and Motivation

'The starting point of all achievement is desire. Keep this constantly in mind. Weak desire brings weak results, Just as a small amount of fire makes a small amount of heat'.

- Napoleon Hill

'A constant struggle, a ceaseless battle to bring success from inhospitable surroundings, is the price of all great achievements'.

- Orison Swett Marden

Some General Information on Stress

Stress is recognised as the number one killer today. The American medical association states that stress is the cause of 80 to 85 percent of all human illness and disease every week. 95 million Americans suffer some kind of stress related symptom for which they take medication.

American businesses lose an estimated $200-$300 billion dollars per year to stress related productivity loss and other cost. To put this in perspective, this amount is higher than the total cost related to all strikes and the net profit from all Fortune 500 companies!

In women, stress has been linked to fatigue, hair loss, bad complexion, insomania, disruption of the menstrual cycle, low libido and lack of orgasm, among others. Women risk more serious problems such as high blood pressure and heart disease.

Young people grow old faster with stress studies reveal that stress reduces the power of your immune system. Studies show that in women the abdominal fat increases with stress. Stress increases heart rate and blood pressure. It changes the inner lining of our blood vessels, making our blood more likely to clot. Stress may change the way cholesterol is handled by our blood vessels and, in doing so, may increase plaque formation. A study of 5,872 pregnant women in Denmark showed that women who are under moderate to high stress in the last stages of pregnancy are 1.2 to 1.75 times more likely to give birth prematurely.

These facts obviously are worth noting and are definitely a cause of our concern, before we decide to face and manage stress in an integrated manner without losing out on life and living.

What is Stress? Definition (Ref A. 8)

- "Stress is the non-specific response of the body to any demands made upon it" - Dr Hans Selye, father of stress studies - 1951
- "An adaptive response to an external situation that results in physical, psychological, and/or behavioral deviations for organisational participants" - Fred luthens, organisational behavioral scientist.
- Doctors define that stress is the breakdown of the coping mechanisms of the body and the mind.

Examples of Stress

- Your car about to get involved in an accident- You escape at the last moment.
- Job related stresses like an unreasonable boss, too much work, unreasonable customer, being passed over for promotion.
- Relationship induced events such as marital problems, death of a spouse, divorce.

- Money related problems such as not being able to return a loan.
- Health problems such as a serious illness.
- Psychological and emotional problems such as thinking of the results of the examinations expected, a performance appraisal pending, an operation for which you are you are getting ready-causing a lot of anxiety. The above can trigger sleep induced disorders which in turn causes a 'domino effect' resulting in more stress.
- Self-induced pressures like when you think that you are not performing well and may be fired from your job.
- Conflicts such as choosing between jobs, choosing among partners while planning to get married, Moving to a foreign country leaving friends and families

Examples of major Life Events which are stressful and their ranking according to a scientific study.

Thomas Holmes and Richard Rahe, developed a list of major life stressors. These are listed in descending order below, beginning with the most stressful event. Only a few few in the list are mentioned below, to enable the reader to understand the issue.

1. Death of a spouse
2. Divorce
3. Marital separation
4. Imprisonment
5. Death of a close relative
6. Personal injury or illness
7. Marriage
8. Fired from a job
9. Marital reconciliation
10. Retirement
11. Illness of a relative

12. Pregnancy
13. Sexual problems
14. Birth or adoption
15. Business readjustment

There are many more in the list of stressful life events of Dr Homes and Dr Rahe. All are not mentioned here by the author.

Classification of Stress(Ref B. 10)

Stresses can be classified into the following four categories for clarity in understanding their nature and 'dealing' with them by anyone who faces them and has to cope.

1. According to Effect

1. Positive(Eustress) - "sukha" in sanskrit
2. Negative (Distress) - "dukkha" in sanskrit
3. Neustress - indifference to stress

2. According to Intensity

1. Life threatening - *e.g.* A terminal illness like cancer
2. Non-life threatening - *e.g.* An examination

3. According to levels

1. Extrinsic - At the organizational level
2. Intrinsic-At the individual level

4. According to Source

1. Adjustment stress
2. Adaptability stress
3. Confusion stress
4. Conviction stress
5. Ego stress
6. Situational stress
7. Frustration stress

Sources of Stress - 'Stressors'(Ref B. 10)

The following are the most common sources of stress which people encounter in their lives.

(a) Physical - Pollutants, noise, cold, heat

(b) Social - Death of a family member, loss of job, fights in family etc.

(c) Psychological -Frustration, guilt, worry, fear, self-pity, anxiety etc.

(d) Negative "Self-Talk"

(e) Chronic negative thinking leads to distress and eventual illness.

(f) Hopelessness. This leads to chronic depression

What needs to be appreciated is the fact that once the sources are identified, we can prevent being stressed out by combating the sources rather than the effects of the 'stressor'.

Our Body's Reaction to Stress- General Adaptation Syndrome - (GAS)

1st Stage-Alarm Reaction: A number of chemicals including Adrenaline release, body tenses up, heart beats faster, breathing becomes harder, eyes dilate etc. .This is called the 'fight or flee' syndrome. This is done by nature to protect us, if something bad happens. Once the cause of the stress is removed, the body will go back to normal.

2nd Stage-Resistance or Adaptation: If the causes are not removed, more hormones are released causing blood sugar and BP to go up. The adrenal cortex (outer covering) produces hormones called corticosteroids for this resistance reaction. Overuse by the body's defense mechanism in this phase eventually leads to disease. If this adaptation phase continues for a prolonged period of time without periods of relaxation and rest to counterbalance the stress response, sufferers become prone to fatigue, concentration lapses, irritability and lethargy as the effort to sustain arousal slides into negative stress.

3rd Stage Exhaustion: In this stage, the body has run out of its reserve of body energy and immunity. Mental, physical and emotional resources suffer heavily. The body experiences "adrenal exhaustion". The blood sugar levels decrease as the adrenals become depleted, leading to decreased stress tolerance, progressive mental and physical exhaustion, illness and collapse.

The hypothalamus-pituitary-adrenal (HPA) chain of command has served humans well as a means of survival for thousands of years.

However, for those suffering from chronic anxiety and depression this process malfunctions. Continual stress early in life disrupts the cycle. Instead of shutting off once the crisis is over, the process continues, with the hypothalamus continuing to signal the adrenals to produce cortisol. This increased cortisol production exhausts the stress mechanism, leading to fatigue and depression. Cortisol also interferes with serotonin activity, furthering the depressive effect.

Continually high cortisol levels lead to suppression of the immune system through increased production of interleukin-6, an immune-system messenger. This coincides with research findings indicating that stress and depression have a negative effect on the immune system. Reduced immunity makes the body more susceptible to everything from cold and flu to cancer.

Thus, very often, people with prolonged stress may contract diseases related to immune deficiency and may even die of these diseases. The death does not come from stress itself. What happens is that the body loses all its resistance in its effort to ward off the stress. Thus the persons die of immune deficiency causes such as infection, cancer etc. So, it is very important that we recognise the causes for stresses and remove the causes to maintain a healthy lifestyle.

Warning Signs of Stress (Ref B. 10, B. 11)

Stress is a good teacher. When a person is going through intense stress, the signs appear in the person in various forms such as physical, emotional, cognitive and behavioral. Some examples are given below which are illustrative and not complete.

1. Physical Signs and Symptoms of Stress-examples

Increased heart rate, pounding heart, elevated blood pressure,

Sweaty palms, tightness of the chest, neck, jaw, and back muscles, headache, diarrhea, constipation, urinary hesitancy, trembling, twitching, stuttering and other speech difficulties

2. Emotional Signs and Symptoms of Stress-examples

Irritability, angry outbursts, hostility, depression, jealousy, restlessness, withdrawl, anxiety

3. Cognitive/Perceptual Signs and Symptoms of Stress-Examples

Forgetfulness, preoccupation, blocking, blurred vision,

Errors in judging distance, Fantasy life, Reduced creativity, Lack of concentration, diminished productivity, lack of attention to detail.

4. Behaviral Signs and Symptoms of Stress-examples

Aggressive behaviors (such as driving - road rage, etc.), increased alcohol or drug use or smoking, carelessness, Under eating, overeating,withdrawl, listlessness, hostility, accident-proneness. nervous laughter, compulsive behavior and, Impatience

The Effects of Stress on Systems in the Body

It is necessary to understand that stress is affecting us before they become 'chronic' and lead to 'serious health problems' which can sometimes be 'life threatening'. The following section gives a list of Health Disorders or Illnesses which are a result of prolonged stresses in individuals. The list is frightening to the reader, nonetheless, very informative and improves our awareness regarding the seriousness of managing stress without losing health.

Central Nervous System-Anxiety, Depression, and Fatigue

Cardiovascular System - Impaired heart function, angina, Constriction of the peripheral blood vessels, blood pressure.

Digestive system - stomach upsets, ulcers, diarrhea, gastritis, and Irritable bowel syndrome

Respiratory System -Asthma

Musculoskeletal system - Tension in skeletal muscles and joints, backache and muscular aches, pains degenerative diseases like arthritis

Immune system - weakened defenses, with lowered resistance to infections, viral illnesses (often due to a depleted immune defense system), allergies, Cancer

Endocrine System - menstrual disorders, thyroid disorders (underactive, overactive, thyroiditis,) adrenal hypo function

Reproductive system - infertility, impotence

General - Tissue degeneration, acceleration of aging process

Stress and Performance (Ref B. 10)

Research reveals that performance in a work situation improves up to a certain situation till the stress is enjoyable and positive, called the 'Eustress' and beyond that point when the stress is excessive and distressful, the performance starts waning till it reaches a point of exhaustion and collapse.

Stress at Work Place - Job Stress (Ref B. 10)

Judy Marshall and cary cooper have researched on job stress immensely. Their findings on the "Sources" of job stress are mentioned below briefly.

- Factors intrinsic to job - Work over load, too much travel etc.
- Role in the company - Role ambiguity, Role conflict etc.

- Relationships - With the boss, subordinates, peers etc.
- Career development - Stagnation, lack of security etc.
- Organisational structure and climate - lack of trust, lack of belonging etc.
- Extra-organisational sources - social change, technology change, family issues etc.

Coping with Stress (Ref B. 10, B. 11)

Having understood how prolonged stress can damage the body and the mind completely, it is time for us to discuss ways to cope with stress or in other words, 'Manage Stress' so that we stay healthy. There are three ways by which human beings try and cope with stress.

They are:

1 Defensive coping

2 Dysfunctional coping

3 Direct Coping

The following paragraphs explain these methods briefly.

Defensive Coping

The stressed individual uses unconsciously his/her ego-defense mechanisms which prevent loss of his/her self-esteem.

Examples:

- Denial, repression, regression, projection, withdrawl, compromise, fantacy, day dreaming dysfunctional coping

The affected individual resorts to extreme kinds of behaviour which can be termed 'Dysfunctional'.

Examples such as :

- Maladaptive coping behaviors which lead to increased smoking, too much coffee, alcohol addiction and drug addiction, Tendencies to commit suicide.

However, the best way to cope with stress is through direct-coping discussed in the following sections.

Direct Coping - Positive

The methods suggested below form the crux of 'Stress Management'. The following are the broad classifications.

1. Change your thinking
2. Change your behaviour
3. Change your life style
4. Change from person to a spiritual person.

They are discussed more elaborately in the following sections of the paper.

1. Change Your Thinking

Reframing-Positive Thinking: A negative situation may be looked at as an opportunity to learn and hence becomes positive. Example-when a student gets less marks in the exam, he learns that he can do better, works hard ad scores well the next time. People can learn from health problems and improve health, through better diet and exercises and habits.

Change Your Behaviour

Be assertive - Learn to say no to negative things and suggestions from others.

Get organised/time management - Instead of rushing and getting stressed for time, better priority fixing and time management will help ease pressure and tension.

Ventilation - vent out emotions in a positive way without offending people,

Humour/laughter - humour and laughter are the best medicines for health and cheer. Be with people who are cheerful and not those who sulk and complain and look sad.

Diversion and distraction - While going through difficult

situations, think of diverting your attention to positive things to manage stress. During difficult work periods, a week end trip to a holiday resort nearby will help.

Change Your Lifestyle

Diet-Physical Exercise-Relaxation: A good balanced diet rich in protein and vitamins and less in fat, combined with regular exercises like walking, jogging or cycling, playing some active games or workout in a gym with enough rest and relaxation will do the trick of ensuring good physical health and simultaneously a calm mind.

Playing with Children

Nothing like playing with small children to bring all the lost qualities in life. Learning from children is part of the challenge. We have to become forgiving and enthusiastic like children to regain our lost motivation to live well.

Bio-Feedback

Take feedback from one's own body- mind responses from time to time and adjust the health routines.

Drink Water

Drinking at least 2 to 3 liters of water a day is a must.

Deep Breathing

While tension mounts up, a good deep breath, helps ease the tension. Regular pranayama in the morning or evening improves all the body systems and tones up the entire health.

Nature Walks-Travel

Nothing like a week-end trip to a nearby hill station or a beach resort. A simple trek in the woods nearby will rejuvenate and bring energy back in to you.

Imagery Hydrotherapy

Imagining a nice river or a sea or a water fall relaxes the mind.

A Warm, Hot Bath

This relaxes the body and mind completely after a hard day at work.

Music Therapy

Listening to good, soothing music or singing oneself is a great stress buster.

Reading

Reading Good books before going to bed or during holidays at home is a great way to gain knowledge as well as means to focus the mind and stay calm, relaxed and confident.

Sleep

Sleeping six to eight hours a day .is a must for recharging the body and mind. Too much sleep can make one dull and lethargic.

Yoga and Meditation

The benefits of yoga are acknowledged internationally now. Mixing yoga and meditation with normal forms of exercise in a judicial way without overdoing both is a healthy way to live disease free.

Change from A Person in to a Spiritual Person

The latest research on the positive effects of 'spirituality' in the mind, body and the spirit of a person reveals enormous benefits ranging from prevention to complete 'Healing' of dreaded diseases like heart ailments, arthritis, back, joint problems and cancer.

The author believes that regular prayer, reading spiritual literature, listening to enlightened spiritual leaders and gurus should become a way of leading a happy, healthy and peaceful life for any individual. The author is personally experiencing this in his life while he also adopts the direct and positive methods of managing stress discussed in the preceding sections. The TV and Internet Media have made access to 'Spiritual Knowledge' easy nowadays. One has to be careful in choosing good sources to obtain spiritual wisdom which will come only through regular practice of what is taught by a great guru and a lot of 'Self-Inquiry'.

Stress and Motivation

The functional methods of coping with stress are known to us now. They are methods like doing exercises, relaxation technique, laughing, playing with children, yoga, meditation, travel, prayer, spirituality and so on as mentioned in the foregoing discussions.

We are going to discuss here as to how we can make all the above coping happen in our lives with regard to stress only if we bring in an awareness that 'Motivation' is again a key attitude. We need to maintain in order that we can make the above techniques yield results for us for effective stress management

Role of Motivation in Stress Management

Any issue related to stress and the technique used to manage stress has to be perceived and brought within the gamut of the motivation paradigm.

An example will help.

Let us say that a person decides that keeping physically fit through exercises is a good way to cope with stress. First of all, he or she has to re-define this situation as a motivational issue by understanding the need involved, the goal or the objective to be reached and the drive or the desire to be sustained till the goal is reached.

So far as physical exercises are concerned, the need in any person is physical fitness, the goal is a strong and a fit, muscular body and the method is regularity I exercise, say four or five times a week, followed by healthy, fat free food and rest in adequate measure.

Once the need - drive-goal model of the physical exercise issue is understood by the person, it is easier for him or her to relate to the motivational challenge involved in sustaining the habit .

Let us take another example, say meditation with a view to manage stress related issues in daily life. To bring in motivation in o the habit of meditation on a daily basis, one has to understand the need to use meditation to achieve the end objective of coping with stress. The need in this method can be perceived as relaxation which is purely a physical or mental comfort or a security need or in the case of a more evolved person to understand self which is an actualisation need. For a third person, it can be a combination of security and actualisation.

People may join group meditational programs in which case the need to belong to such groups of like-minded individuals also gets merged with the need to relax and to actualise. The goal in this case obviously is health, physical, mental and spiritual. The type of meditation, the duration daily etc., will constitute the path and decide the drive the individual needs to develop in order to make meditation habitual in yielding the end result of coping with stress and leading a more meaningful, joyous life.

In short, the author wishes to tell the reader that while he or she tries to manage stress through the various techniques mentioned in the foregoing paragraphs, it is important that he or she remembers to understand the need-drive-goal issues in the methodology which will improve the effectiveness of coping and the possibility of attaining the end results desired.

Conclusion

Methods of managing stress were discussed elaborately in this chapter. Many or all of those techniques are known to people nowadays owing to the presence of Stress Experts, Therapists and Gurus of various categories including the spiritual gurus in large numbers.

The author has tried to add a new 'dimension' to the idea of 'Stress Management' by telling the reader and making him 'understand' that without 'recognizing' the 'motivational aspect' of stress management by appreciating the needs involved, the methods used, the 'drive' needed to sustain and the goals that are in stake while people manage stress, the consequences of lasting health, happiness and peace of mind may not be completely achievable. If the reader appreciates this, the author has succeeded in 'communicating' the message intended to be beneficial to all in maintaining health and harmony in life.

References

Books

A. 8. Dr. Anjali Ghanekar, "Organisational Behaviour."

"Concepts and Cases," Everest Publishing House, Pune, Eighth Edition, 2002.

Journals, Articles

B.10. Dr Viswanathan Gopalan, 'Stress Management and The Science of Living,' VIPSAR, Indore, ISSN Journal, 2013 June.

B.11. Stress Management - Helpguide.org.

www.helpguide.org/mental/stress_ management_ relief_ coping. htm.

9

Motivation and the Purpose of Life

'Each Soul is potentially divine. The goal is to manifest this divine within by controlling nature, external and internal'

Swami Vivekananda

'Prayer is not asking. It is a longing of the soul. It is daily admission of one's weakness. It is better in prayer to have a heart without words than words without a heart.'

Mahatma Gandhi

Motivation and The Purpose of Life (Ref B. 2, B. 5, B. 6)

In the previous chapters we have covered the principles, philosophies, theories and practical information pertaining to motivation in personal life and in work life. We have discussed in detail the importance of motivating knowledge workers in work places for improved productivity and innovation. We have discussed the role of motivation in perceiving, coping and managing stress in an exclusive chapter for the benefit of the reader.

This chapter is totally dedicated to the understanding, analysis and interpretation of the concepts discussed in the previous chapters with regard to the biggest dilemma all human beings face in their lives at some point of time or the other. That is this according to me the biggest question each individual asks himself or herself many times and never gets a full answer is, "Who am I and what is the ultimate purpose of life for which I was brought on to this planet called earth?" A common person asks this question, a rich man, a politician, a scientist and even a saint pursuing a spiritual path asks this question often.

We are not going to provide an answer directly to this question because I believe that first of all I am not capable of answering it. I neither have the complete knowledge and wisdom to answer this question which falls in to the realms of the unknown and unmanifested and I feel it is the job of the most enlightened spiritual masters to provide a completely viable answer to the question of the ultimate purpose of life both for the believer and the atheist as well.

I intend to share with the reader, knowledge worth assimilating by him or her so as to make life more meaningful and purposeful. I intend telling you my thoughts and views on how we can look at certain critical issues which all human beings experience and need to experience without understanding why. I would say primarily there are a few vital realms of knowledge and experience which all the human pursuits apparently aim to achieve, fulfill and complete. They are, according to me, the following:

1. The concept of love.
2. The concept of happiness.
3. The concept of eternal joy.
4. The concept of peace.
5. The concept of God, creation death and enlightenment.

I intend to facilitate the reader to look at these issues purely from the point of motivation to live life well and not expect answers which will aim to unravel the mysteries of the cosmos. The following discussions, hopefully, will help improve the awareness of the reader to understand the role of motivation in the larger issues in life and the purpose.

The Connection- Love and Motivation

Love, some spiritualists, most of them or all of them say, is the ultimate bond between God and a human being. Some psychologists like Maslow perhaps interpret love as a deep actualization need of the human being which he or she encounters in several circumstances in his or her life and yearns to fulfil that need by achieving something worthwhile and satisfying that deep-felt need in the process. Common man who is neither a spiritualist nor a psychologist believes that love is a feeling or an emotion which affects him repeatedly in varying degrees in multifarious simple and complex situations in life. Several times he does not know how to deal with it without losing its purpose, role and meaning in life.

The author believes that love is a need felt by human beings as well as the other living beings like some animals and birds. Love is emotional in character and requires a goal to quench and fulfil it

We will be dealing with human love and not venture in to animal love or bird love since we do not have sufficient knowledge in these areas of understanding. We will confine our discussions to love among human beings viewed from a motivational angle and the conclusions we draw in order that we can sustain it lifelong.

Some Examples will Help the reader

Let us say some one remarks in an excited voice, "I love ice cream". What this guy is trying to communicate is that he has a 'deep liking' or an 'intense longing' for ice cream because when he eats ice cream which is his goal, his intense longing for ice cream translates in to happiness and satisfaction accompanied by an invigorated body condition and a filled stomach which hopefully feels nice too.

In this case, there is this need of love for ice cream, there is a drive and there is a goal namely eating ice-cream. The interpretation by the author is that this is intense craving for food which satisfies the eater physically and psychologically and there is a lot of motivation in achieving it.

Then Where is the Problem?

The problem lies in the fact that the goal is very short term and lasts for a short time till the hunger crops up again when the act has to be repeated by the eater for a repeat happiness. This way, soon the addiction for ice-cream sets in and the love turned craving becomes lust and addiction. The situation is clinical and totally dysfunctional. The end consequence could be obesity, a disease like diabetes and a host of other related illnesses for the ice-cream addict.

Let us take another example in which the goal becomes a long term goal or a 'Vision' commonly called a 'Dream'. I will try and explain through this example how motivation can be sustained right through the process for a long time bringing happiness to the individuals involved.

Let us say that the 10 years old son of a Tennis Player also likes to learn the game. The father, who is a good club level player, decides to encourage his son. He develops a vision that his tiny 10 years old son will one day become the national champion in Tennis and perhaps internationally famous. This the father decides, he will help his son to achieve this dream within the next 10 years. This decision prompts the father to develop a drive, clear cut strategies and plans. The father decides to put his son through an extensive coaching programme so that he can participate in district, state level junior tournaments during the next 4 years and then move him on to senior ranking tournaments in the national circuit, then decide how to take this process forward when his son develops his full potential to grow in to a top grade player.

Obviously, the father needs to decide about the finances involved, the trips to various tournament sites in the country with his son to provide the constant support the little boy requires and so on.

I would end the story by quickly saying that the father's dreams are bound to come true as he has chalked out a motivational process with clear goals and necessary drive understanding his and his sons needs fully well. The needs are based on the 'Love' for the game which is at an 'Actualisation' level for both the son and the father. It also indicates the 'Love' the father has for his son and the efforts he is willing to put in to sustain that love with his own commitment. The commitment to sustain is already there and the father and the son are bound to remain motivated and enjoy the journey to the very logical end.

It goes without saying that difficulties are bound to arise as the boy grows in to a full-fledged player. It goes without saying that he has many goal posts or mile stones to cross. If the hurdles to the progress are overcome without losing hope, sustaining motivation, the dream of the father and in turn the son will certainly come true.

What I would like to point to the reader is that in the above example that the need is a 'Growth need' addressing the 'Love' for the game which is an actualization need in the Maslow's need hierarchy and the goal is long term, hence a vision breakable in to smaller achievable yearly goals and the drive is genuinely stemming from both the individuals dreaming the end goals or the achievements planned for. Obviously, the 'LOVE' we talked about includes the love of the father for the son and the love of the son for the father and their love for the game. There is total synergy in the process and completion.

I would conclude my analysis of this concept of love from a motivational perception by saying that as long as the love needs are working at actualisation levels and the goals are long drawn out and the drive is sustained with commitment, the end result will be fulfilment, achievement and happiness. Else the process can be short lived, unsustained and repetitive not yielding permanent satisfaction and happiness.

The Connection - Peace, Happiness and Motivation

The motivation concepts which we discussed with regard to love apply equally well with regard to our needs for peace, happiness and joy. We will try and convince you that as long as these needs are understood as actualisation needs, and as long as the goals are long term visions and as long as the drive is genuine and sustained, the experience of peace, happiness and joy will be sustained by the individuals in pursuit of those dreams or else, the experiences can be fleeting, short lived or none.

Here again some examples will help the reader understand what I am trying to tell.

Let us take the example of a person who faces problems in life with regard to personal life issues like an unhappy marriage or professional issues like an unfulfilling job or a difficult boss. Let us say that instead of coping with these challenges positively as suggested by the author in the chapter on stress management, the candidate resorts to dysfunctional ways of coping. Let us say the guy starts drinking alcohol every time he needs to get peaceful or happy, he does achieve the goal momentarily. However, the moment the effect of alcohol wanes, the frustrations return more severely and soon the guy become an established 'Alcoholic', begins to lose health and mental balance. He is soon down the decline path and the slide soon leaves him broken in every way.

The reader is knowledgeable enough in motivational principles by now to understand that alcohol is a short term solution even if it momentarily satisfies the needs for peace, happiness and joy. It ruins health, happiness and peace in the long run despite the individual being driven by these needs and is committed to the cause. The short term goal that too, a wrong one, namely alcohol as the goal post, results in a disaster for the individual who ends up as a total wreck and a failure in life.

What then is the answer to this question of lasting peace, lasting happiness and lasing joy? It is very simple. All that we need to do is to replace the goal 'Alcohol' in the above example, by some good, tangible, long term goals called visions. They can be 10 years visions, 20 years visions or better still life long visions. I will tell you how.

We can say that this guy who became an alcoholic in search of peace and happiness can reframe or redefine his motivational model with a long term goal such as 'I will work to help Alcoholics kick the habit and thereby contribute to bringing happiness and peace in their lives. I will be committed to this vision of mine'. He can set a vision for himself like, 'I will work to save the poor children abandoned by society by providing health, shelter, education and love'. He can make declarations like 'I will work to repair my broken relationship with my dear wife and children whom I neglected for years because of ......'. He can make statements like 'I will love all human beings around me and treat them as equals and contribute through love to bring happiness and peace in their lives'.

These modified vision statements when put in to action by the individual brings about 'Transformation' in him from day one and sets him on a path to the fulfilment of his 'Actualisation needs of Love, Peace, Happiness and Joy'. It is quite possible he encounters frustrations and back slide on the way. But sufficient courage, commitment and drive to work towards the defined missions, visions, mile stones and goal posts on the way transforms the mere individual from the 'Ordinary' to the 'Extra-Ordinary' or even 'Enlightened' as the 'Spiritualists' will articulate the change.

In the following section we will discuss our quest for God realisation looked at from a motivational perspective. The views are absolutely mine. They are never intended to criticize or hurt any religious beliefs or sentiments.

The Connection- Reaching out to God and Motivation (Ref A.9, B.5)

The most complex question any human being on this planet can ask is this. 'Who am I? Where from did I come? When I die what happens to me?' The questions most of us ask ourselves are 'Am I the body and the mind or is there a thing called the spirit living in this body-mind-matter?'

I have been a scientist, engineer, a management teacher and researcher for long. I have learned and been led to believe that all these questions can be answered if we focus our attention to the world and the cosmos around us. What fascinates us is the vastness of the space around us, the countless galaxies, the stars and planets that are visible to our naked eye, and through the telescopic instruments we use and those that are not visible but we know that they exist. We are also perplexed at the duration of time these stars and planets have existed and the amount of energy that is constantly transmitted from one cosmic body to another in various forms such as light, radiation and other types of electro-magnetic waves.

All the religions in the world try and address this issue which has been bothering mankind for ages namely, "How was this Universe or the Cosmos created? If there is a creator, is he different from the creation?' Questions regarding the oneness of the creator with His creation or his separate existence from lives and the matter and the space he created led to views like the 'Brahman' and the 'Atman' are separate indicating the Duality or Dwaita concepts or views like they are the same indicating the Adwaita concepts in Hinduism. Concepts like the 'Holy Spirit' passing through and directing us in a positive direction every moment of our lives are inherent to the ideologies from religions like Christianity which depict Christ as the Son of God sent to the world and sacrificed on the cross to pay for the Sins of Mankind and resurrected back to the heavenly abode of God to join the Holy Spirit and God for eternity. These truths and beliefs are meant to elevate mankind to think in terms of the manifested and un manifested forms of energy from which the Cosmos evolved.

Without going in to the comparisons of these spiritual or religious ideologies which aim to reach man to God which is a very noble purpose, I would only address one issue in this book. That is, "To pursue a spiritual path for enlightenment, Salvation or Mukhthi, does Human Motivation play any role in the lives of individuals? If so, how do we understand those mechanisms of motivation which will lead us to those ultimate objectives of enlightenment, joy, happiness, eternal bliss and lasting peace?"

In the motivational context, we redefine the issue as follows. Eternal Bliss, Happiness, Joy and Peace are to be understood as incomplete actualisation needs in human beings to begin with. Then God realisation or connecting to Cosmic Energies known and unknown as the ultimate purpose in and beyond life as the vision. The picture begins to become clearer to us at once.

To complete the picture of the above motivational road map to freedom, we just need the 'Drive Factor' and a means to sustain it lifelong. From my experiences in my life and my pursuits to spirituality and liberation from the bondages of birth, I have realised the following methods can be used to generate and sustain the drive. They are:

1. Keeping the body and the mind in good condition through exercises and yoga as a preparatory step– Need for health and drive.
2. Yoga as a way of life – Need for health and drive.
3. Meditation – Focus on goal- short term plus long term.
4. Faith and Prayer as a regular means– Focus on God-the goal.
5. Seeking the support and blessings of a Guru-Need-drive-goal attainment.
6. Reading and listening to Scriptures from all religions and understanding that all of them lead you to the ultimate creation and the creator-Need-drive-wisdom-goal attainment.
7. A lot of reflection on the self and the cosmic energies to focus our attention to this eventual knowledge and wisdom that we are an extension of the cosmic energies around us.

Need for Wisdom-drive-Goal of Self-realisation and Enlightenment

Many more methodologies or Kriyas can be adopted but I would say that we should stay focused maintaining the drive for reaching out to the Ultimate. It is possible that we 'back slide' and encounter 'frustration' on the way owing to barriers known and unknown many of which we discussed in an earlier chapter. If we climg on, believe and retain the motivation, the drive, the faith and the purpose, I am sure we will eventually succeed and reach the lotus feet of God, The Almighty, one day.

References

Book

A.9. Sadhu Vaswani, 'The Heart of the Cita', Gita Publishing House, Pune

Journals, Articles

B. 1. David C.Mclellend,' "Managing Motivation to expand Human Freedom," American Psychologist,1978

B. 2. Dr. Viswanathan Gopalan, "Motivation and Its Relevance to Productivity." Thesis for Ph.D, Pune University, 2001

Dr Viswanathan Gopalan, "Motivating Knowledeg Worker". ISSN-Journal Symbiosis, 2012

Dr Viswanathan Gopalan, "The Significance of Motivation with Regard to Productivity," ISSN Journal, Amity University, Lucknow, 2014

10

Summary

'I count him braver who overcomes his desires than him who conquers his enemies; for the hardest victory is over self'

- Aristotle

'Before the throne of the Almighty, man will be judged not by his acts but by his intentions. For God alone reads our hearts'

- Mahatma Gandhi

We have come to the concluding chapter of this book. So far, I have tried to share my knowledge with the reader, most of all the knowledge I have inherited with regard to motivation and its role in our lives. The knowledge the reader gained includes the definition, meaning and importance of motivation, theories on motivation, barriers to motivation and how to overcome them, how motivation impacts our personal lives, research data on motivation in work places and the most important needs that affect productivity in work places with the author's own recommendations for productivity improvements, stress and its correlation to motivation, means of coping with and combating stress.

A full chapter was devoted to the topic of 'Knowledge Management' and the issue of motivating the 'Knowledge Worker. The chapter at the end dealt with the actualisation needs of individuals in life namely Love, Peace, Happiness and the desire to reach God or to attain a state of enlightenment and freedom and the connect among these needs from a purely motivational perspective.

Before I conclude, would like to share with you the real life story of one of the greatest Human beings the world has witnessed in modern times. She is an inspiration to not only those of us who are sighted and well, but those who are visually impaired.

You guessed it right. I am going to share with you the story of Helen Keller, the woman who could neither see, nor hear and speak from childhood, who overcame all those difficulties and became one of the greatest women leaders of all time, social activist and author whose life story must be read by each and every one of us if we really mean to understand the meaning of 'Motivation'.

I chose the life history of Helen Keller for one reason. I have been working as a key member of a Non-Profit, NGO which has been helping to educate, provide literacy for visually handicapped children in India. During these past few years, I have also met some of the most enlightened, socially contributive, visually challenged people of eminence in India, whose personal and professional lives, have been filled with achievements and contributions to humankind that cannot be comprehended by even people with vision.

The Story of Helen Keller (Ref B. 9)

Helen Adams Keller was an American author, political activist, and lecturer. She was the first deaf blind person to earn a Bachelor of Arts Degree. The story of how Keller's teacher, Anne Sullivan, broke through the isolation imposed by a near complete lack of language, allowing the girl to blossom as she learned to communicate, has become widely known through the dramatic depictions of the play and film *The Miracle Worker*. Her birthday on June 27 is commemorated as Helen Keller Day in the U.S. state of Pennsylvania and was authorised at the federal level by presidential proclamation by President Jimmy Carter in 1980, the 100th anniversary of her birth.

A prolific author, Keller was well-travelled and outspoken in her convictions. A member of the Socialist Party of America and the Industrial Workers of the World, she campaigned for women's suffrage, labour rights, socialism, and other radical left causes. She was inducted into the Alabama Women's Hall of Fame in 1971.

Early Childhood and Illness

Helen Adams Keller was born on June 27, 1880, in Tuscumbia, Alabama. Her family lived on a homestead, Ivy Green that Helen's grandfather had built decades earlier.

Her father, Arthur H. Keller, spent many years as an editor for the Tuscumbia *North Alabamian*, and had served as a captain for the Confederate Army.[Her paternal grandmother was the second cousin of Robert E. Lee.[Her mother, Kate Adams, was the daughter of Charles W. Adams. Though originally from Massachusetts, Charles Adams also fought for the Confederate Army during the American Civil War, earning the rank of colonel (and acting brigadier-general). Her paternal lineage was traced to Casper Keller, a native of Switzerland. One of Helen's Swiss ancestors was the first teacher for the deaf in Zurich. Keller reflected on this coincidence in her first autobiography, stating "that there is no king who has not had a slave among his ancestors, and no slave who has not had a king among his."

Helen Keller was born with the ability to see and hear. At 19 months old, she contracted an illness described by doctors as "an acute congestion of the stomach and the brain", which might have been scarlet fever or meningitis. The illness left her both deaf and blind. At that time, she was able to communicate somewhat with Martha Washington, the six-year-old daughter of the family cook, who understood her signs; by the age of seven, Keller had more than 60 home signs to communicate with her family.

In 1886, Keller's mother, inspired by an account in Charles Dickens' *American Notes* of the successful education of another deaf and blind woman, Laura Bridgman, dispatched young Helen, accompanied by her father, to seek out physician J. Julian Chisolm, an eye, ear, nose, and throat specialist in Baltimore, for advice Chisholm referred the Kellers to Alexander Graham Bell, who was working with deaf children at the time. Bell advised them to contact the Perkins Institute for the Blind, the school where Bridgman had been educated, which was then located in South Boston. Michael Anagnos, the school's director, asked 20-year-old former student Anne Sullivan, herself visually impaired, to become Keller's instructor. It was the beginning of a 49-year-long relationship during which Sullivan evolved into Keller's governess and eventually her companion.

Anne Sullivan arrived at Keller's house in March 1887, and immediately began to teach Helen to communicate by spelling words into her hand, beginning with "d-o-l-l" for the doll that she had brought Keller as a present. Keller was frustrated, at first, because she did not understand that every object had a word uniquely identifying it. In fact, when Sullivan was trying to teach Keller the word for "mug", Keller became so frustrated she broke the doll.

Keller's big breakthrough in communication came the next month, when she realized that the motions her teacher was making on the palm of her hand, while running cool water over her other hand, symbolized the idea of "water"; she then nearly exhausted Sullivan demanding the names of all the other familiar objects in her world.

Formal Education

Starting in May 1888, Keller attended the Perkins Institute for the Blind. In 1894, Helen Keller and Anne Sullivan moved to New York to attend the Wright-Humason School for the Deaf, and to learn from Sarah Fuller at the Horace Mann School for the Deaf. In 1896, they returned to Massachusetts and Keller entered The Cambridge School for Young Ladies before gaining admittance, in 1900, to Radcliffe College, where she lived in Briggs Hall, South House. Her admirer, Mark Twain, had introduced her to Standard Oil magnate Henry Huttleston Rogers, who, with his wife Abbie, paid for her education. In 1904, at the age of 24, Keller graduated from Radcliffe, becoming the first deaf blind person to earn a Bachelor of Arts degree. She maintained a correspondence with the Austrian philosopher and pedagogue Wilhelm Jerusalem, who was one of the first to discover her literary talent.

Determined to communicate with others as conventionally as possible, Keller learned to speak, and spent much of her life giving speeches and lectures. She learned to "hear" people's speech by reading their lips with her hands—her sense of touch had become extremely subtle. She became proficient at using braille and reading sign language with her hands as well.Shortly before World War I, with the assistance of the Zoellner Quartet she determined that by placing her fingertips on a resonant tabletop she could experience music played close by.

Companions

Anne Sullivan stayed as a companion to Helen Keller long after she taught her. Anne married John Macy in 1905, and her health started failing around 1914. Polly Thomson was hired to keep house. She was a young woman from Scotland who had no experience with deaf or blind people. She progressed to working as a secretary as well, and eventually became a constant companion to Keller.

Keller moved to Forest Hills, Queens, together with Anne and John, and used the house as a base for her efforts on behalf of the American Foundation for the Blind.

Anne Sullivan died in 1936 after a coma, with Keller holding her hand.[19] Keller and Thomson moved to Connecticut. They traveled worldwide and raised funds for the blind. Thomson had a stroke in 1957 from which she never fully recovered, and died in 1960.

Political Activities

Keller went on to become a world-famous speaker and author. She is remembered as an advocate for people with disabilities, amid numerous other causes. She was a suffragist, a pacifist, an opponent of Woodrow Wilson, a radical socialist and a birth control supporter. In 1915 she and George Kessler founded the Helen Keller International (HKI) Organisation. This organisation is devoted to research in vision, health and nutrition. In 1920 she helped to found the American Civil Liberties Union (ACLU). Keller traveled to 40 some-odd countries with Sullivan, making several trips to Japan and becoming a favorisite of the Japanese people. Keller met every U.S. President from Grover Cleveland to Lyndon B. Johnson and was friends with many famous figures, including Alexander Graham Bell, Charlie Chaplin and Mark Twain.

Keller was a member of the Socialist Party and actively campaigned and wrote in support of the working class from 1909 to 1921.

Keller joined the Industrial Workers of the World (the IWW, known as the Wobblies) in 1912, saying that parliamentary socialism was "sinking in the political bog". She wrote for the IWW between 1916 and 1918. In *Why I Became an IWW*,[24] Keller explained that her motivation for activism came in part from her concern about blindness and other disabilities:

Writings

Keller wrote a total of 12 published books and several articles.

- At age 22, Keller published her autobiography, *The Story of My Life* (1903).
- Keller wrote *The World I Live In* in 1908, giving readers an insight into how she felt about the world.]*Out of the Dark*, a series of essays on socialism, was published in 1913.
- When Keller was young, Anne Sullivan introduced her to Phillips Brooks, who introduced her to Christianity, Keller famously saying: "I always knew He was there, but I didn't know his name."
- Her spiritual autobiography, *My Religion*, was published in 1927 and then in 1994 extensively revised and re-issued under the title *Light in My Darkness*.

Later life

- Keller suffered a series of strokes, in 1961 and spent the last years of her life at her home.

- On September 14, 1964, President Lyndon B. Johnson awarded her the Presidential Medal of Freedom, one of the United States' two highest civilian honors. In 1965 she was elected to the National Women's Hall of Fame at the New York World's Fair.
- Keller devoted much of her later life to raising funds for the American Foundation for the Blind. She died in her sleep on June 1, 1968, at her home, Arcan Ridge, located in Easton, Connecticut, a few weeks short of her eighty-eighth birthday. A service was held in her honor at the National Cathedral in Washington, D.C., and her ashes were placed there next to her constant companions, Anne Sullivan and Polly Thomson.

Posthumous Honours

- In 1999, Keller was listed in Gallup's Most Widely Admired People of the 20th century.
- In 2003, Alabama honoured its native daughter on its state quarter.The Alabama state quarter is the only circulating US coin to feature braille.
- The Helen Keller Hospital in Sheffield, Alabama is dedicated to her.
- There are streets named after Helen Keller in Zurich, Switzerland, in Getafe, Spain, in Lod, Israel, in Lisbon, Portugal and in Caen, France.
- A preschool for the deaf and hard of hearing in Mysore, India, was originally named after Helen Keller by its founder K. K. Srinivasan.
- On October 7, 2009, a bronze statue of Helen Keller was added to the National Statuary Hall Collection, as a replacement for the State of Alabama's former 1908 statue of the education reformer Jabez Lamar Monroe Curry. The statue represents the seminal moment in Keller's life when she understood her first word: W-A-T-E-R, as signed into

her hand by teacher Anne Sullivan.

The above life story of Hellen Keller is downloaded from wikipedia a free encyclopedia available on the Internet. - Author

Conclusion

I wish to conclude this book by saying one thing. If someone as challanged as Helen Keller was when she had virtually no access to all the conveniences of technology, could achieve so much and contribute so profoundly to society, what prevents us in this 21st century where every modern means of reaching out to the world is available to us at the click of a button.

There is nothing that can prevent us from staying motivated, setting visions and goals to achieve in life, enjoying the whole journey with zest and happiness till we come to rest in eternal peace at the feet of the Almighty.

References

Journals, Articles

B.7. Helen Keller- Download from Website, Wikipedia-The free Encyclopaedia, 2014

Bibliography

A. References on Motivation, Productivity and Management-Books

1. AH.Maslow, "Motivation and Personality", Harper & Bros, Newyork, 1054

2. D.C.Mc Clellend, "The Achieving", D.Nostrandco. Inc, Princeton, N.J.,1961

3. D>M.Mcgregor, "The Human Side of Enterprise," McGraw-Hill Book Co.Inc.,Newyork,1960

4. Frederick Hertzberg, "Bernard Mausner & Barbara Shydermann," The Motivation to Work", 2nd Edition, John Wiley and Son. Inc, Newyork, 1959

5. Shyam Gokhale, "Personnel Management and Organisational Behaviour",Publisher,Mrs.Susheel Gokhale,1st Edition, 1961

6. Keith Davis and J.W.Newstrom, "Human Behaviour at Work-Organizational Behaviour," Mcgraw-Hill, Newyork, 1989

7. Fred Luthens, "Organisational Behaviour",Mcgraw-Hill Inc., Newyork,1995

8. Dr Anjali Ghanekar, "Organisational behaviour, Concepts and Cases," Everest Publishing House,Pune,Eighth Edition, 2002

9. Sadhu Vaswani, 'The Heart of the Cita', Gita Publishing House, Pune.

B.References on Motivation, Productivity and Management-Journals

1. David C.Mc Clellend, "Managing Motivation to Expand Human Freedom," American Psychologist, 1978.

2. Dr. Viswanathan Gopalan, "Motivation and Its Relevance to Productivity." Thesis for Ph.D,Pune University, 2001

3. Fred Luthens and Robert Krietner, "The Management of Behavioural Contingencies," Personnel, July 1974

4.Frederick Hertzberg, "One More Time,How do you Motivate Employees," Harvard Business review, Selected Articles, Reprint, Motivation, 1970.

5. Dr Viswanathan Gopalan, "Motivating Knowledeg Worker". ISSN-Journal Symbiosis, 2012

6. Dr. Viswanathan Gopalan, "The Significance of Motivation with regard to Productivity," ISSN Journal, Amity University, Lucknow, 2014

7. Article on Hellen Keller, Download from Website, Wikipedia-The free Encyclopedia, 2014

8. Thomas Muster - Wikipedia, the free encyclopedia *en.wikipedia.org/wiki/Thomas_Muster*

9. Thomas Muster – Tennis Players - Tennis - ATP World Tour *www.atpworldtour.com/Tennis/Players/Mu/T/Thomas-Muster.aspx*

B. 10 Dr Viswanathan Gopalan, 'Stress Management and the Science of Living', VIPSAR, Indore, ISSN, Journal, 2013 June

B. 11 Stress Management - Helpguide.org *www.helpguide.org/mental/stress_management_relief_coping.htm.*